SEX EDUCATION AND THE SPIRIT

Sex Education and the Spirit

*Understanding Our Communal Responsibility
for the Healthy Development of Gender
and Sexuality within Society*

LISA ROMERO

STEINERBOOKS | 2017

2017

STEINERBOOKS

An imprint of SteinerBooks / Anthroposophic Press, Inc.
610 Main Street, Great Barrington, MA 01230
www.steinerbooks.org

LIBRARY OF CONGRESS CONTROL NUMBER: 2017931608

ISBN: 978-1-62148-191-1 (paperback)
ISBN: 978-1-62148-192-8 (eBook)

Contents

This book was written in gratitude to my Developing the Self—Developing the World colleagues, who dedicated their time to bringing this work to students, parents, and teachers in order to support community wellbeing.

INTRODUCTION

One of the significant changes we are faced with in our present time is a collective shift in relation to our understanding of gender and sexuality. Because these particular changes are present in the life of every human being that walks the earth, we cannot avoid reflecting on this individually. Even if we feel that these questions have no impact on our personal lives, we are nevertheless facing a collective change that will affect us all in some shape or form. It has affected, and will continue to affect, the educational systems; it has affected, and will continue to affect, our community life—and thereby it will affect each one of us in some way.

As the inevitable changes occur in our development as a collective humanity, we are often faced with the question: Is this change progressive? Do all the changes that take place as we evolve as individuals, as communities, and as humanity—do all of these changes actually serve our growth and development? We may also ask: How can we understand what is taking place in the wider community in the light of having and maintaining an individual spiritual life?

Whenever there are changes on a world scale, individuals with a spiritual perspective will try to observe these changes through the eyes of spiritual activity and ask: Where is there an opportunity for deeper understanding to offer spiritual insight into the changes taking place? Can these changes lead us to a greater manifesting of spiritual impulses in the world?

At this stage, we have around seven billion people living on planet earth, and it may be interesting to consider that the overwhelming majority of these individuals recognize a spiritual life of some sort. Some do this through religious worship, some through collective beliefs about an understanding of spiritual existence; others come to a spiritual life through comparatively small groups, and still others have a very individual connection to what they recognize as spiritual realities.

As diverse and varied as individuals are within any faith or understanding of the spirit, there are several overlapping and unifying links. One example of an important link, or collective recognition, is the understanding that a human being is more than just a physical, material body.

In the light of the spirit, regardless of a person's school of thought, religious education, leaning, or acquired faith, we can recognize a general agreement that the human being extends beyond the external, material body. All agree that we are not only this physical substance, that we're not only chemistry.

In many spheres of life and human society, there are differing points of view. These differing points of view can lead humanity into great conflict. We see that conflict as it manifests between different religions, we see that conflict between different races, and we see that conflict between different classes. Regardless of the race, religion, or class we are born into, we all encounter the conflicts that arise in the realms of gender and sexuality.

Of all these realms, the conflict that takes place in the realms of gender and sexuality could be seen as the most divisive of all; and if we prove ourselves capable of truly understanding each other in this realm of life, then the social understanding required to overcome our intolerance toward diversity in gender and sexuality would help us in the conflict-laden divisions of all the other realms of life. No group can remain untouched by the changes that are taking place collectively at this time in the realm of gender and sexuality.

In the late 1990s, I presented the first of a series of courses on male–female studies in the light of spiritual life. When I look back on what I was able to present then and compare it with what I am presenting now, I recognize how different the work has become—and not only how different it has become, but how important it has become. How we live and relate to one another as human beings has consequences not only for our outer life but also for our inner, spiritual life.

I have learned that if—in the context of our community life and educational systems—we limit individuals' development by means of conditioning that is no longer relevant to the spiritual needs of our times, we are thereby limiting their capacity to engage with the progressive spiritual forces working with humanity.

As we evolve and develop as individuals, our understanding of the spiritual world should evolve and develop as well. We have moved on from the concept of the "all seeing God" who alone is responsible for all the details of our lives. We now participate in life with greater individual responsibility for carrying out what we individually perceive to be true, harmonious, and good according to our spiritual schooling.

Each spiritual epoch of human evolution has its unique task in supporting our communal progression in the direction of developing love and freedom. In and through us, the world is taking shape. In and through us, humanity is potentially becoming a greater and fuller representation of the living divine life.

In this age, we will need to see each other anew. In this age, we will need to begin to treat each other as individuals—to look upon the other as an individual with certain capacities, talents, and gifts that can contribute toward an ever-progressing and evolving society—a society that is not devoid of the spirit, but that is working to reveal the spirit more fully as it evolves.

Many who are on the path of inner development ask questions about gender and sexuality. What is the place of sexuality in a deeply spiritual life? And how does sexuality affect our spiritual life? Through many years of educating others about gender and sexuality from the point of view of the spiritual life, together with the work of educating about the meditative path, I have come to recognize the importance of meeting young people in a new way.

Gender- and sex-education of young people today now needs to come primarily from the realm of social education—in the form of wisdom lived and embodied by the adults around them. The basic biologically and physiologically focused sex education classes that they commonly receive are not enough to provide the complete education needed for a positive impact on the physical and soul health of the developing child. The social element of education is very important, as all young people are already being educated about sex and gender through social media. We have no choice but to meet this with an education that supports the growing young people in a health-giving way, and that adds truly social pictures as a balance to the often one-sided influences of these media.

There are many ways to convey the wisdom of the spirit. In this small work, I've attempted to seek a universally human "common ground" in this very human enquiry of the place and right understanding of sexuality and gender in the light of the spirit. Our collective community consciousness will naturally affect how we educate the next generation as well as whether we will succeed in working together to create a healthy form of gender- and sex-education.

I

GROWING UP MALE AND FEMALE

Our spiritual life is our deep belief and understanding of existence, which even affects our very physical existence. Our spiritual beliefs and principles inform and form our inner soul life. What lives in our inner life is the foundation of what arises as our community life and the social life or social structure of our community. Our spiritual life plays a major role in how we cultivate our inner world, and the same is true of the outer influences of our collective society, which play back upon our inner world. This is a principle that the individual adult can change, but that the child cannot. All children are educated by the community around them, and in light of this fact we are all educators of the next generation.

Although our inner world is unique to each one of us and to our experience of our own individuality, it is through our community life that individuals may express themselves and contribute to the collective community consciousness—and thereby, contribute as well to the evolving of humanity. Even though one person's spiritual life may differ strongly from that of another, there are some abiding principles that we have in common, which serve to build bridges among us in the context of our collective community life and collective community consciousness.

One of the foundational pictures that most people share through cultivating a spiritual understanding of the world is that there is a spiritual or divine aspect to the human being. And it is in this light that we recognize all human beings as "brothers and sisters"; it is in *the spirit* that all are born equal. Regardless of our status or social standing in the community, we all partake in a divine life that dwells within us, and we are all equal in the eyes of God, or spirit.

Among the various spiritual movements and religions, we can see another aspect that we all have in common—that is, there is a divinity, a divine aspect, or a quality of consciousness that is above and beyond, or more than, the consciousness we carry in ourselves as individuals. This divine spirit, God, or great consciousness is something we can strive to know, commune with, or become one with.

The understanding that we can grow closer to our God, to the divine, or to the greater consciousness, leads us to explore the way in which we may practice our relationship to the spiritual world. This is another common denominator among humanity, expressed in that each faith, religion, or spiritual movement presents certain conditions, laws, or guidelines that are to be fulfilled in order to deepen the individual's relationship with the divine. Individuals take upon themselves these conditions in order to be able to unite more and more with the great consciousness, the divine, God, or the great spirit of their faith or group or particular path.

In some faiths, there are many laws or conditions, whereas in others there are comparatively few. Within each faith or spiritual group, every individual practices these laws or conditions to varying degrees, on an individual basis. Some pray or meditate only rarely; some pray or meditate daily; and some pray or meditate several times a day. There is no single religion, faith, or spiritual group in which every individual involved carries out identical ways of practicing or relating to their path, even though we all have common threads that align us to our particular stream of spiritual life.

These common threads, which are seen throughout the various spiritual groups, can also be seen to have their influence on how developing children learn about community life and the social structures around them. As an educator, these factors are quite fundamental to working with young people from the perspective of understanding what is happening within them at various stages of their development, and from the perspective of how best to educate them about everything that belongs to the social life.

The image that there is truly a spiritual world, and that we are participants in this spiritual world, is not an uncommon concept—however, the way each of us relates to the spiritual world can be very different. This is what we refer to as the ability to reach a state of unity with the divine. In some religions, it might be called "communion"; in other religions, it is the sense of "oneness," of "nirvana," or a "unification of our consciousness with the divine," and so forth.

Regardless of which name it is given, this spiritual reality is accessible to us because it is a reality that we carry with us from the higher regions of the spiritual world. Although we may lose this natural "knowing" while we are growing

3

into the body, it still lingers for a time in the world of the small child.

Descending, as it were, from the realms of spiritual life, the child slowly becomes "earth-ripe," and then, gradually, becomes a fully contributing member of the community's collective consciousness. Until then, they live more strongly, albeit unconsciously, between the governing principles of the spiritual world and the experiences of the surrounding physical world. Still under the influence of the abiding realities of spiritual life from birth to around age seven, the child of this age primarily learns by means of the spiritual principle of "unity and connectedness with the surrounding world." Then, from age seven to fourteen, the child moves on from this principle of unity and learns more from the laws or conditions governing the community life that they are growing into.

During the first seven years of life, we often hear consistently that children learn through imitation, that they are imitators—that children imitate the world around them. But what does it mean to be an imitator? From our earthly point of view, we could think it simply means "copying," as that's what "imitation" usually means. From a scientific point of view, it's seen as the effect of mirror neurons. From a spiritual point of view, what the young child is experiencing is a residual spiritual ability. It is likewise a quality that one can experience in the depths of spiritual activity. And that quality is: *I unite my consciousness with the other's consciousness—I'm not separate from the other.* In this realm of the physical world, I'm here and you're there; there is an absolute separation. In the realm of the spiritual world, everything lives *within*; I am *in*, or unified with, this or that being or con-sciousness. When we say that the child is an imitative being, what this truly means is that the child's consciousness is still penetrating the other forms of consciousness around it. It is as if the customs of the earlier life in the spiritual world are still working on, long after the child has left that world. It's not actually a matter of "copying" the other person in the way that we usually think of "copying"; rather, the child's consciousness is still working out of spiritual laws that it experienced in the realm of unification and communion.

It's very hard for us as adults, considering the strongly self-orientated way that we stand in ourselves, to imagine the small child as living within their environment. We see children engaged in the world around them; we see them screaming and shouting—they want what they want, they're stamping their feet. But actually, their consciousness is mingling with their surroundings, and this is where they imitate from; it's not just copying. This is something that lives in the experience of the young child as a resounding reality between birth to age seven—for the young child, although born into the world, still resounds with the image of "unification with the other."

Today, when the issue of teaching gender and sexuality is entering the educational system, we have to ask: How can we truly teach this? When we recognize that the primary way the young child learns is through imitation, then we clearly don't want to intellectually teach gender and sexuality from ages zero to seven; rather, we should *live* what we want them to learn. The true education for them is going to be what moves in their environment. We already know that the education of the small child—what becomes deeply ingrained in the small child—is what they have experienced around them. Research is showing that by the time the child is six years old, the community's embodiment of gender stereotypes will be inscribed upon them already.

This principle is true of all processes of social education for the young child. What lives in their environment becomes their true education. Their deeper learning comes through the environment that they imitate, not through intellectual teaching. They learn through *living in the other*, not through mere copying. And they live especially intensively in the soul skin of those adults around them who play a strong role in their lives. Even though their body is separate, their soul is not yet enclosed within themselves. This can be daunting for the primary adults in the child's life, because the adult may recognize that in order to truly educate freely and not pass on their individual biases and errors, they will have to learn to perceive what lives within themselves. When I try to perceive the errors that live in me, then, although the child continues to experience the errors, they also experience my good will toward transforming them.

In the next phase of child growth, from ages seven to fourteen, they have moved on from living unconsciously in the soul skin of the other, and now live more within their own temperament and constitution—but they are still working with and learning out of spiritual principles, though now these are principles of a different quality. They look toward the authority figure, believing this authority to be a representative of truthfulness in which they can trust, because that is the reality of the spiritual world. It is the reality of the divine spiritual world that all authorities are authorities of truth, worthy of trust. Again this can be daunting for the primary caregivers, having to present what is true and trustworthy to the child. Because of the inherent power that outer authorities have over the child at this age, it is especially important that the education of sexuality and gender be brought in a health-giving, harmonious way. It is a common experience for young people to be shocked by exposure to pornography at an early age. As educators, we have to bring harmony and health to some of these detrimental influences that "other educators" such as social media, peers, and technology have on the young child.

Because these influences have already entered the world of the child, we therefore need to bring certain harmonizing pictures to the child—and we have to bring them in a way that is relevant to where their consciousness happens to be. There are two principles that are common to nearly all religions and spiritual movements: one is that there is a divinity that we are connected to, and the other is that certain guiding laws resound within the child until around age thirteen or fourteen, when they become what Rudolf Steiner terms *earth-ripe*.[1]

Today it happens in the fourteenth year that the incarnated child, who was once living in union with the divine principles and laws, looks upon the surrounding world as it is and recognizes that there is a great discrepancy between the life of the spiritual world and the world that human beings have made on earth. This discrepancy can spark a rebellion toward the outer world, especially if the young person does not find adults in their community who are striving to bring spiritual truths into earthly existence. If children cannot see their community working toward bettering the world, then adolescents can go into rebellion against the community. Such rebellion can be a diverting force lasting until their late twenties, and in some cases it continues to divert the individual from having any impact on the progression of society as a whole.

There is a healthy subconscious clash between young people and the world around them, because this world is far from the spiritual truths that they know, deep within their souls, to be possible for humanity.

The ability to perceive the progress of a community is not an outer matter that we can explain to young people. It does not have a single sign that they can look for. Rather, the progress of a community is expressed in our way of engaging with and giving ourselves to the outer world. This may express itself in our love for our task or in our capacity to support others. Adolescents will recognize whether the adults standing before them are giving of themselves or taking for themselves.

As a child begins to enter puberty, we most often consider this from a purely biological point of view. It is seen from the perspective of biological and physiological shifts and hormonal changes. Maturation processes are acknowledged through biology in sex education classes. The change of voice, the growth of hair on the body, the change of smell, the numerous changes taking place within the body and in the emotions of the child—these are spoken of as the direct effects of the change and fluctuation of hormones. These changes, culminating in the onset of menstruation and the maturation of the male voice, are rightfully seen as biological processes.

However, puberty also has a soul–spiritual aspect, which is of far greater consequences for the evolving of society. If we consider that the individual enters into the bodily vehicle, gradually descending into it from the spiritual world, then from a soul–spiritual perspective, puberty means that the child is now becoming a participating member capable of beginning to transform the outer earthly world. They begin to be able to give to the world through the qualities and capacities that they have brought with them.

Each generation and each person is bringing something new into humanity. Although this may not be clearly perceived by the community—as puberty is only the very beginning of a process of showing who they are and what they are here to give—this beginning is still very important as the child gradually becomes a contributor to the collective consciousness. In this way, the adolescent also becomes the responsibility, to a certain extent, of the wider community.

It is through this "soul puberty" that, in the adolescent, the new impulses descending from the spiritual world come together with the older forms in an intensified way. Inevitably, there is often a clash between the older forms, which want to maintain things the way they are, and the new impulses that the young people are bringing—especially if what they are bringing isn't acceptable to the established forms of the community.

We often recognize a collision between what young people are bringing with them from the spiritual world to bring humanity forward, and what such individual expression comes to meet in the community that wishes to mold children in accordance with its values. This clash can cause not only outer rebellion, but also inner disturbances of the soul such as loathing and depression, especially if the adolescent is unable to have genuine encounters with adults who are working toward the progress of humanity. Even subconsciously, young people are clashing with the world around them in certain ways because what they are "allowed" to bring is far from the spiritual truths that they know to be possible.

How we meet the young people during their time of "earth-ripeness" is indicative of the extent to which our collective community consciousness has evolved from the older forms into the new impulses that they are bringing.

For many young people, there is a certain absurdity in the fact that in our time, we still focus on the genitals only as a means of reproducing. When we impose upon them our desire to make their puberty into a special event (perhaps because the event of puberty has lived in our own souls in an imbalanced way), this does not support their process of integrating this very natural bodily experience.

In our time, it is much more important for a young person that we focus on their unfolding inner capacities as unique individuals: the qualities they carry, what they have to bring to the world, and how they are affecting the world.

Biological puberty has its place, and needs to be presented to young people in a natural and harmonious way—in a way that reflects the quality and nature of their generation. We also need to address the soul–spiritual aspect of puberty that is now awakening in the adolescent. Inviting them into community life is a step toward focusing on the true potential of individuals. There is nothing more helpful for young people, especially between the ages of fourteen to sixteen, than to be engaged with interest in the world around them. Through this, they can begin to assess where they can find a place in the world in light of what they are bringing out of themselves, as well as their perception of how other human beings are bringing their individual gifts and capacities into the world.

It takes several years of this process of both learning from and "giving of themselves" to the world before young people can self-will their inner capacities into the world in the way adults do.

By the time children are around thirteen or fourteen years old, the vast majority of them are biologically capable of being parents; however, the capacity to be responsible for the wellbeing of other individuals requires more than biological readiness.

Even in the biological aspect of puberty, we see the "signature" that the human being is not just a physical body. We recognize that the higher activities of our humanness require more than merely reaching puberty, and we recognize that this is something different from past cultural tendencies.

In the distant past, in all cultures puberty meant that the individual was fully ready for the responsibilities of community life. It meant that they were ready for marriage, ready for childbearing, or for work. It is now more common for children as young as nine years old to be menstruating. It is clear that there is a difference between bodily puberty and soul puberty; there is also a difference between soul puberty and the capacity for conscious, autonomous development.

As we continue to unfold our spiritual development, we see that, soul–spiritually, we are not ready for these responsibilities just because our body is. Again, we have collectively begun to recognize the evolving human being; we now see that more is required of the individual than simply the physiological changes of puberty.

Throughout human evolution, we have progressed through different "soul ages" or "epochs" during which the focus of our evolution as individuals changed from one soul capacity to another. Rudolf Steiner describes these epochs more thoroughly in his book *An Outline of Esoteric Science*.[2] In our current epoch—which could be characterized as the "consciousness soul" or "self-consciousness soul age"—we recognize that self-consciousness is the most significant aspect of reaching the capacity to take upon ourselves the responsibilities that come with adulthood. We no longer look solely to the physical body as our indicator of adulthood, but rather we look upon the physical body merely as the beginning of the next stage of the adolescent's development—the stage that, when supported, will lead to healthy adulthood.

If we look into the soul nature of young people, we can recognize that *on a physiological level*, puberty arises in various ways and at different ages for each individual—further, it arises under the influence of a combination of hereditary, dietary, and environmental factors. However, *on a soul level*, puberty is perceived when individuals begin to bring something within them into the world around them. This occurs for all adolescents around the age of fourteen, regardless of the onset of physical puberty.

First, teenagers struggle with being able to communicate clearly what lives in them, and how they wish to bring it into the world. We sense that their inner life is very raw and vulnerable, yet it is expressed in them in varying degrees of two polar opposites: vulnerability and roughness. Even within the same individual, they are at times hardly able to get a word out, and at other times rampantly talkative, or anywhere in-between. All are awkward and lacking confidence in their beginning attempts to relate to the wider world with soul intimacy.

This "something" that they are to bring into the world is not what has been conditioned into them; it is what lives in them from their earlier process of participating in the spiritual world. Human beings each bring with them the capacity to transform and evolve the world around them, even if only in a small way. In soul puberty, we begin to see who this individual is who is now awakening out of childhood and into an adolescence that is not determined by their upbringing.

Here lies a certain indication for the new "coming of age" and rites of passage that the young person needs to experience in our "self-consciousness soul age." It is all about the capacity to bring what lives in the depths of the inner world into relationship with the outer world. They seem to be attempting this by themselves already, using social media as their platform. If this is the only venue available to them through which to express themselves to the community, then they are also left with the cruel and harsh criticisms of their peers and others who are often not looking to embrace them but rather to deface them.

An ideal form for this new process to reach expression is that young people choose a mentors from whom they would like to learn, or by whom they would like to be supported in their work on a project. There will be more impact on the young person in terms of experiencing the embrace of the wider community if the mentor is not a family member or a close friend of the parents. This allows for the independent development of a relationship between the adolescent and another community member, which can be experienced as a bridge to community. A further step would then be a presentation given to the wider community. It would be at this time that the adults in the community could recognize that this child is now theirs to look out for. In truth, it is the *community* that takes the adolescent into adulthood; we cannot rely exclusively upon the parents or the bonds of blood any longer.

As community members, we can witness those individuals as members of the community, and in our hearts we can believe (even if we cannot perceive) that they have something to bring to the community and that it is our duty to support them in bringing it.

In ancient traditions, these rights of passage needed to be very different, as they were living in a different age of human soul development. During the evolution of the human being, we have needed to work on different aspects of what needs to be evolved in the world around us. How we are now, as human beings relating to the world around us, is the result of the evolving stages of human progress in earlier cultures. For instance, in the past we would not have been able to differentiate the inner world into defined realms of thinking, feeling, and willing capacities. This development needed to be cultivated over time. In order to refine in this way the inner life that we now all take for granted, other human beings in the distant past needed to give themselves over to the cultivation of new stages of inner development for the sake of future world evolution.

The fact that we have a vibrant capacity to experience the world in the way we do is due to the previous work of human beings who have developed that capacity. And the fact that we have an ability to be effective in the world around us from out of our individual will is again a result of that capacity having been developed by others in earlier times.

We can look back upon the ancient initiation rites and observe these capacities being developed. When people only had the subtle beginnings of the capacity to experience the world and to confront the outer world as a self-enclosed being, these capacities were developed further by some individuals, who were taken into a training in which they were instructed to observe and experience the external events of the natural world and to allow these events to work upon them. They then began to develop the inner capacity to experience the world around them more deeply through allowing experiences arising from the outer world to penetrate their inner world, awakening inner imaginations. These students learned to bring the feminine forces into development. Others of the tribe worked against the outer world, forcing and forging their own will against the outer elements, thereby creating clear and distinct boundaries between themselves and the outer elements. They learned to bring the masculine forces into development. These initiation rites were not so much a "coming of age" celebration, but a progressive task that the adolescents were brought into once they were able to withstand them and participate in them.

In the ancient past, we needed to work toward differentiating will forces from feeling experiences, as they were soul activities in "seed form," still as yet ungoverned by the individual. Men and women were separated from each other during their respective trainings in initiation in order to provide a certain task for all of humanity to come.

Masculine forces were developed by many people using their will to go up against the elements, and in so doing they were able to clarify their relationship to the world around them. From this came the capacity to define what is outside of me and differentiate this from what *is* me. The capacity to have an impact on the outside world allowed us to develop what we now all take for granted: an individualized will.

Similarly, the feminine forces developed through the life of feeling experiences. It began with the fine forms of an imaginative capacity, but over time it developed into the ability humanity now has as an *experiencing being*, a being able to experience the qualities behind the outer appearance of things.

We all live with the capacity to experience (through our feeling life) what the other is revealing to us, as well as the capacity to bring ourselves creatively into the world (through the will). We have these capacities thanks to the progressive evolutionary striving of those who came before us. As individuals, we can access both the feeling and the willing capacities that now exist in all human beings, although in varying degrees from individual to individual.

Because of this dedication to the progress of humanity on the part of earlier human beings, we can all, through our individualized will, have an experience of a spiritual element within us, which we may call the "eternal masculine," the healthy sense of self. Through the ability to give ourselves up to outer impressions, we are all able to have an experience of achieving the "eternal feminine," the capacity for devotion.

What we take for granted today as a capacity of inner experiencing in which the outer world can penetrate us and moves us, is a result of the developmental striving of human beings in times past. What we take for granted as the capacity to influence the world around us, to embody an individualized will, is the result of the work of past human beings to develop this capacity.

With this knowledge, we can continue to feel deep gratitude and respect for those ancient cultures that today still shine through the indigenous peoples of the world, and we can support these peoples in maintaining their culture.

Once adolescents become "earth-ripe"—though by now they have been conditioned by the laws of the community in which they have been brought up—they still maintain access to genuine spiritual knowledge. We need to support them in bringing the depths of their hearts and minds into the world around them, because it is in these depths that spiritual substance still resounds.

This of course does not mean merely having opinions about things—we all do plenty of that in our peripheral personality. Rather, it means being able to express and share some of our deepest thoughts and feelings about the way we wish to see the world progress, and also to express these thoughts and feelings through our actions.

We do not know adolescents if we think that, left to their own inner world, they will merely strive toward self-indulgence and self-gratification. In the depths of their being, they are deeply concerned about the welfare of humanity. We know that if we can allow them to develop fully and healthily between the ages of fourteen and twenty-one, then these young people will want to make an impact in service of a positive future for humanity.

Although we often think that we need social programs in order to effect positive change in society, what we actually need is a new social attitude—an attitude that recognizes that we're not just a body. We are still so attached to an external, materialistic way of thinking that we immediately put the other in a box the moment we meet young people. Instead, what we need to do is grasp the spiritual reality of the individuality as a being that utilizes the masculine and feminine forces cultivated in ancient times—forces that now express themselves in all human beings to varying degrees, regardless of sexual characteristics.

Ancient rites of passage along the lines of gender are not in keeping with the blossoming acknowledgment of

individuality that we now see emerging in our culture. However, we do need some rites of passage that say, "Yes, you're
part of this community, you have something to bring to it,
and we are looking forward to helping you bring it!"

Rudolf Steiner stated that an intensive pursuit of spiritual
understanding "will lead humanity to overcome gender in
itself," and will lead us to rise up to the level of our pure
spiritual being or essence, "which is beyond gender, beyond
the personal—to rise to the purely human" (Rudolf Steiner,
"Women and Society").[3]

What is taking place through the body's biological changes
is a natural occurrence; it needs to be spoken about with
openness and ease. It is something that everyone needs to
pass through in order that the body may become an adult
body. There is no need in our times to make this all about
being a man or being a woman, for this is no longer the spiritual task. The young people have no need for us to separate
them in order to talk to them about puberty. In fact, separating them leads to greater prejudice in our times and shows
a lack of understanding on our part for the generations that
are coming.

If we focus so strongly on the outer appearances of the
children, and divide and separate them according to their
sexual characteristics, we thereby place an increased importance on the outer body. The more focus we place on the
external body, the less we are able to see and truly perceive
the individual that is beyond gender and sex. This tendency
to separate individuals according to their sexual characteristics will present greater problems in the future, as many

individuals do not classify themselves—whether biologically or inwardly—in binary terms of "male and female."

It may be due to social conditioning that one child or another may find conversations about puberty embarrassing. The way we approach educating young people around this theme can be very helpful to them in overcoming their discomfort. But this is one of the most natural aspects of being human: Our bodies have to grow up. Understanding this growth and development as a natural phenomenon takes away the mystery around the sexes and allows us to communicate as individual to individual. As simplistic as it seems, we should ask ourselves: What social preparation does this individual need in order to grow into relationship with others in a mature and adult way in the future? Should it be that only those with a female body understand menstruation, and only those with a male body understand the forces behind ejaculation? The problem of the sexes is a socially conditioned one. We have to overcome these past forms of conditioning and prove that they are overcome through the way we engage in practical life. We do a disservice to the nobility of the human being when we reduce it to the status of a mammal through focusing on the mere biology, and through this, unconsciously proclaiming that human beings are just their bodies.

> The harmony above the sexes can only be found in so far as the two sexes raise themselves to that level. If, therefore, by making use of the knowledge to be gained from spiritual science we could enable the reality beyond the sexes to take effect in practical life, then the problem of

the sexes would be solved. (Rudolf Steiner, "Man and Woman in the Light of Spiritual Science")[4]

As has been mentioned, puberty of the soul is just the beginning of the individual's capacity to bring the harmony and laws of spiritual reality into earthly life. It is not until the awakening of the self-conscious consciousness between the nineteenth and twenty-first years that the self-transformative capacity can begin to be expressed by the individual. We can then freely and independently govern the forces arising in our soul and take hold of the outer world, directing it and seeding it with the gifts we have already acquired in our spiritual life. We can also begin, through the transformation of our own soul, to acquire more gifts and more capacities with which to serve the transformation of the world.

There is a very valuable time for young people, between the ages of fourteen and twenty-eight, when they can easily be diverted from bringing their true capacities by the materialistic outlook prevailing in the world. They may even end up giving up the quest toward a future of growth and change. However, when young people are given the freedom to express and unfold themselves, they are not as easily swayed by the empty materialism that is pounding them from the outside. It is the adults in the community that serve as pillars of support to these young people. Evidence shows us that the positive effect of an adult's care is even more significant when someone who does not *need* to love them—a community member who is not of the blood bond—shows interest in an adolescent's world. When this happens, the adolescent can come through the darkest of trials. It can be very difficult for parents to be role models for their own adolescents, as many adolescents are trying to individualize and separate themselves from their family. It requires a community to bring up adolescents through those vulnerable years.

It is always uncomfortable to look back and recognize that what I thought in the past, and what I lived in the past, is no longer progressive and of the future. This is the nature of individual revelation. Our "personal particular self" would still like to defend our old ways because we always want to be right. However, when we step back from our personal particular preferences and consider what is right for the whole, what is right for all, then we have to look toward a form of guidance on a deeper level than what merely relates to us personally. We have to consider what makes sense now as a spiritual reality unfolding in the world. What is being asked of us spiritually at this time? What would be progressive for the human being at our stage of evolution? What is the initiation task of this epoch?

What capacities are we being asked to develop now? What legacy are we leaving for the future of humankind? An answer is revealed in picture form in the image of how we support those who are going through puberty. The ability of those young people to communicate what lives in the depths of their hearts and minds through their speech is not only essential for their own development, but also for the future development of humankind.

Why is our ability to communicate from the depths of our hearts and minds into the world around us so important for this next stage of human development? The human soul entering into the material world already has an understanding of spiritual life, even when this understanding has been conditioned or covered over in a materialistic way. It is the *human soul* that feels and conveys qualities that are not born from a materialistic way of thinking or attitude.

If we are to prevent our entire world from descending into materialistic ways of seeing and being, then we need to be able to convey what is taking place within us, as our deepest experiences, into the world around us. This is not the task of adolescents alone, but at puberty they finally join us in this great task—and, fresh from the spiritual world, they still contain the seed elements of the future that our world needs. If we could see what they carry as a potential of creative energy, we would recognize it to be our task to support them, as a community, in standing strongly in their own individuality so that they may participate in the evolving world.

The wholeness, the completeness of our soul nature, is expressed in our ability to experience our "I am" consciousness. We can *think* and we can *feel*—and therefore experience—the other; and we can *will*, and out of our willing we can change the world around us. The changes that we have seen, which have taken place in the course of the last thousand years—these dramatic, extraordinary changes are also the result of human beings working into the world.

What changes, among those brought into the world by human beings, have had the effect of continuing to serve our spiritual understanding of who we are? And what changes have human beings brought into the world that have had the effect of separating us and dividing us from the understanding that we are also, in part, spiritual beings? Are all the changes a part of our progression?

Each individual is born out of the spiritual world and into the earthly life. Each bears the impulses for transforming the world toward the direction of the spirit. It is in the "I am" that each has its quota of transformative force. What we do with that is our individual responsibility. Will I utilize this capacity to transform the world in order to fulfill personal wants and wishes, to gratify my sensory nature and my egotism, or will I use this force to better the world and myself?

What does it mean to better the world and ourselves? What is the world evolving into, and in what sense are we able to contribute to this evolution? We can gain a lot from looking at what those in the next generation are working with.

We are given certain indications of what needs to come into the world through us when we look into the world around us—when we look to the various spiritual schools and all of what has been esoterically interwoven into the great religions. Through various forms, we are given pictures of human development, and of how we can best grow and serve the great evolving.

One such picture is that we've moved into the "self-consciousness soul age," which is the fifth age of our particular epoch. Every age lasts 2,160 years, which is the period of time for the Sun to transition its position fully in the zodiac as it rises during the equinox from one sign into the next. It is with this periodic transition that great collective change takes place. With this transition from one sign to the next, we could say that the spiritual–creative impulse wants to bring something new into the evolution of humanity. And the spiritual–creative impulse that we know to be essential to the "self-consciousness soul age" is entirely related to *developing the impulses for freedom*—freedom in our thinking, in our feeling, and in our willing individuality.

> In more recent times, the spirits of light have changed their function. They now inspire human beings to develop independent ideas, feelings, and impulses for freedom; they now make it their concern to establish the basis on which people can be independent individuals. (Rudolf Steiner, *The Fall of the Spirits of Darkness*)[5]

But what is so fascinating—if we understand the evolution of humanity—is that this impulse for the independence of the individuality is the reason we are now working in a very new way only 600 years into the self-consciousness soul age. The way the individuality works into the world in our time is quite different from how we would have worked in the immediately preceding soul age, also known as the fourth age or Greco–Roman period. In the fourth age, grouping people according to outer characteristics was useful because it was a stage in leading humanity toward differentiating. In the fourth age, working in the context of special groups was a progressive way of working: separating and segregating individuals according to sex, race, religion, and so forth. We can still see aspects of this existing in our present time, as residual elements from the fourth age. We can also experience it in our language. What was useful for humanity at one time becomes a principle that diverts or causes great struggle at a later time. In this self-consciousness soul age, the spiritual principle at work strives toward creating, supporting, encouraging, and eliciting *individuality* out of the other and ourselves.

Instead of the encouragement of individuality, and the search for a path to the fruition of our individuality through growth and development, young people are encountering an experience of being pulled in two opposite directions by the darker side of this age. We must all face these consequences of the new age, but we first need to be aware of them in order to manage the trials that will confront us.

One of the consequences of the new age that can be experienced as a trial or darker aspect is the emergence of deep changes in our relationship to our own individual soul life. We are becoming more acutely aware of how we experience soul processes that belong to the universally human experience of our time. In the self-consciousness soul age, we are experiencing more intense feelings of loneliness and isolation than ever before, even though there are more people occupying the planet. Our increased self-awareness brings with it a feeling of separation from other human beings; this sense of loneliness or isolation is a growing experience shared by all human beings. Already from age nine, the young child can begin to experience the fact that they are inwardly different because of this growing self-consciousness. Being different is becoming the new normal. Along with this experience, there is often also a fear of rejection and a longing for acceptance. It is at this age that the child will begin to want whatever things the other children in the collective peer group have and want, or they may be experiencing the feeling of not fitting in on a deeper level. The feeling of not fitting in is shared by so many in the depths of their inner world today, even when they fit the so-called socially acceptable gender and sexuality profile. This experience of not fitting in goes hand-in-hand with a sense of longing, as though something is missing in their lives. These three self-consciousness experiences begin quite simply in the nine-year-old, but grow ever stronger as the child enters adolescence. In this age, all of us must learn to bear these inner experiences, as they are signs of the changing consciousness.

When young people realize that these are natural human experiences, then these trials will have a different impact on them from what would be the case if they were to feel that they alone experience such things—or, worse still, that there is something wrong with them because they are experiencing these things. We need to be careful not to cover up these experiences, but to bear them in a way that they may help us to awaken the strength of our individuality.

The other aspect of the trial we face, which pulls us in the opposite direction, constitutes the greatest difficulty facing us in this time. This is the fact that, hand-in-hand with the self-consciousness soul age, we have the most intensified materialistic thinking ever known to humanity. This kind of thinking has the effect of changing the meaning of our concepts so that, for instance, the concept of individuality isn't able to stand for what it truly is. The concept of individuality is no longer understood to represent the spiritual aspect of our being. The true individuality is our spiritual being, comprising who we are as self-conscious beings, as well as our deeper thoughts, feelings, and will activity. Instead of this, our current materialistic thinking is making the individuality into something that is entirely defined and consumed by the externalized self, our outer presentation to the world, who we each are *as a personality*. This materialistic thinking has not only taken hold of those who do not believe in or cultivate a spiritual life, but it is likewise prevalent in all walks of life: everywhere we look, the individual is being condemned to the mere outer self. In a world that glorifies this superficial personality, very few young people are able to find the space to have conversations about what's really going on as an inner experience.

The world loses us through our inner suffering or feelings of isolation, through our feeling rejected and in a state of "missing out"; conversely, *we are lost to the world* in the superficiality and the externalizing of our being, which is implicitly encouraged by the cultural focus on outer personality.

In order to be of true help to others in this self-consciousness soul age, we have to work with the questions: What truly exists as the individuality of the other? How can we help to support that development throughout the trials of modern life? When we understand what truly makes us individual then we will begin to feel reverence for the soul–spiritual capacities that all individuals bring with them.

The central wisdom understood from the spiritual life and the life of the "I am" is something that we must be mindful of when working with others. An educator must always try to stand in the knowledge of the true being of the other person, especially when working with young people. The truth is that their inner nature does not have sexuality; it does not have a gender. In their "I"-consciousness, and in their soul capacities, they are genderless or dual-sexed. There is something important in this truth, because as we stand in the present age, it is now more important than ever that our focus as educators and community members be directed upon the *soul–spiritual* aspect of the human being that we are meeting.

> Of course, a materialistic view of the world and of the human being, which recognizes only what can be touched and seen, will naturally see in man and woman only the physiological differences; and anyone who remains in this materialistic view will simply miss, will simply overlook something that is far greater and more decisive than sexual differences. They will overlook the individuality, which goes beyond gender and is independent of it. (Rudolf Steiner, "Women and Society")[6]

Our task is not to focus on who stands in front of us as a mere external person embodying a certain skin color and certain sexual characteristics. The realization of this fact is one of the tasks of the educator during the self-consciousness soul age. If we go back several hundred years or so, an educator had a totally different task; at that time, one educated only certain people about certain things. This cannot be the truth that is carried forward in the self-consciousness soul age; individuals should now have the opportunity to be educated as they so desire—not according to their outer appearance. However, in the world we experience groups of people who live according to the belief that only certain people should be educated, and only about certain things. We do not need to be teachers in order to be responsible for the education of others, as we are all educating others all the time through our way of being and living, and through our way of communicating and relating to the social life around us.

So even though the impulse that we stand within today has nothing to do with judging and assessing each other according to outer characteristics, the residual tendencies of the past continue to unfold into the world around us. Part of the reason these tendencies continue to unfold into the world around us is that, as individuals caught up in a materialistic view of the world, we are thereby further removed from the reality of who we truly are and of the new impulses we carry within us.

We are caught up in this external picture of the other that originates in the judgmental inclination of the personality, and that grows into very wide and deep divides that continue to inflict pain in the form of the collectivist sentiments of racism, sexism, and other prejudices based on outer appearances. By its very nature, materialistic thinking causes these collectivist errors to perpetuate themselves; they could not be maintained within the atmosphere of the living spiritual element that is working toward humanity. Only materialistic thinking could sustain such judgments based on material qualities.

Humanity is in an evolving process, involving social structures that change according to shifts in consciousness. In the self-consciousness soul age, we are asked to look upon our bodies as an instrument or vehicle. This is not to diminish the vessel of the body, but rather to recognize the true and essential nature of the being that utilizes this instrument.

We can see that the ongoing materialistic tendency of judging and assessing the other according to outer characteristics is serving to place young people in a position whereby they are more focused on the peripheral aspects of themselves. They are awakened into their personality, or peripheral identity—how they appear to the outer world. Their externalized self becomes the fake central self, and in that diversion they actually seem to be further removed from the task of our time and the role they could play in it.

This is a significant aspect of being an educator in the self-consciousness soul age. It is our task to educate in a way that helps those we educate to "carve out" spaces for a genuine, deepened inner life. As an educator, we are doing our task well if we are able *to elicit the individuality* from the other—if we're able to call it forth and make room for all that the individual truly is. That is the task. If we forget for a moment about the *content* of what we are teaching, and if we are yet able to see clearly the *essential inner nature* of the pedagogical task, then we will know how to teach. In fact, it is possible for a teacher to have an absolute grasp of every aspect of the content being imparted—yet lacking the ability to elicit from the other who they are as an individual, to fall short of being a true teacher of our time. This is of course an increasingly difficult task in schools where academic results based on testing are consistently pushed.

Lacking this eliciting ability, not only do we fail to approach the children as individuals, but we also do what we should never do—we try to stuff them full of *our* ideas of who they should be. Where do our ideas come from? They will primarily come from the community we are living in or have been brought up in. If we haven't freed our own thinking, and if we haven't actually awakened something of our own individualized feeling life and will, then our ideas are things that have been inscribed upon us, which we in turn inscribe upon our students, stuffing them with conventional ideas of who they should be.

Though it is not always easy to comprehend from our materialistic way of thinking about the human being, it is nevertheless true that there are actually substantial consequences to teaching young people in this way. One image is that if we were to teach children intellectually—stuffing them with the ideas of the intellect—and in so doing do not call up their individual thinking, their individual capacities, then we affect their ability to unfold the whole of who they are. When we bring our personal selves to bear upon children, then what they are bringing with them from the spiritual world can more easily be displaced. This is something we should think about in terms of the evolution of humanity.

Every generation that is entering into the world comes with creative impulses for the future. So when we stand as parents and educators and think, "I have got to teach you," the reality is that they also have something to teach us.

If certain forces within them are cultivated exclusively, and others are not cared for or cultivated at all, then we create a diversion of those neglected processes. One example of this is when those born in a male body are encouraged not to show their feelings, whereas those born in a female body are encouraged not to show strong will forces. Females are more likely to be prevented from having a tantrum as a child, and males are more likely to be told not to cry. Females are more likely to be comforted when they are emotional than males are. Males are more likely to be coaxed out of the need for comfort. However, we should not jump to the conclusion that we must now push females into stronger tantrums or impose extra comfort upon the males. Each child needs to be met according to individual needs and tendencies, not his or her genitalia. We need to care for the children's individual ways of being and, while holding this in our hearts and minds, contemplate, pray, or meditate on the question: How can I help you to be all that you need to be?

These examples of one-sided behavior toward another human being because of the body they are born into affects the entirety of their development. Neuroscience is showing that, from the moment children are born, we are likely to treat them differently according to the gender of the bodies into which they are born. From this, neural pathways develop in accordance with the particular form of nurturing that the individuals receive. It is evidence such as this that has caused the Australian Children's Association to ask toy shops to not put all the "action toys" in blue boxes on one side of the shop and all the "home-care toys" in pink boxes on the other side of the shop.

The scientific evidence tells us that we are limiting the development of children by conditioning them into a limited range of toys with which they should play. These conditions can be so pervasive that, as they come up against the individuality—which is growing stronger in this self-consciousness soul age—that individualities can begin to feel that they simply don't fit with what is being placed upon them.

It is not the blue or the pink box that is the problem. If we were to look at it in that way, then we would lack a deeper understanding. The true impact resides in all the community's conditioned thoughts that stand behind the colors of those boxes. These thoughts say, "If you are a boy, you'll play with these toys and you will want these things; if you are a girl, you will play with these other toys and you will want these other things." In our current age, in which the capacity of self-consciousness is gathering strength, it must be very disturbing to hear this and to come up against the conditions that are placed upon us simply because we have a body that appears more male or more female.

If whatever the soul wishes to bring into the world is unable to unfold from out of its individual will, then what it intended to bring can be suppressed or diverted from a healthy form of expression. There are three areas in which the diversion will express itself: through the will forces, the feeling–experiencing, or the thinking capacity.

The will is the ground for procreative forces; it is the realm where we individualize and bring ourselves to the world. We do this in various aspects of our lives, including in our sexual relationships. For many, the realm of sexual love does not occupy a significant place in their lives at all; for others, its place in their lives changes over time; and for yet others, it's an important expression of healthy intimacy.

Healthy sensual love is an expression of this will-centered creativity. That is not so say that sexual love is always an artistic act, but only that the qualities of creativity are present. The sexual love that two people share with each other is unique to them; their sexual relationship forms through the two being present to each other in an intimate way each time they connect sexually. This means that each sexual encounter with the other is new—and in being new, it's a part of a creative process of coming-into-being with the other.

> Bodily delight is a sensory experience, not any different from pure looking or the pure feeling with which a beautiful fruit fills the tongue; it is a great, an infinite learning that is given to us, a knowledge of the world, the fullness and the splendor of all knowledge. And it is not our acceptance of it that is bad; what is bad is that most people misuse this learning and squander it and apply it as a stimulant on the tired places of their lives and as a distraction rather than a way of gathering themselves for their highest moments. (Rainer Maria Rilke, *Letters to a Young Poet*)[7]

Clearly, sexual love is not only the primary way in which we continue welcoming the future generations of human beings to the earth; it also is an expression of intimacy between people, and a way of expressing love through the pathway of the senses. For many, it can be the doorway to understanding the more spiritualized aspect of love.

> Sensual love also gradually leads to the highest, purist spiritual love. The soul should transform and order all experiences, and then bear them up to the altar of spirituality. For nothing, absolutely nothing is lost. Sensuousness is the school without which a human being would never come to spirituality. The earth is no vale of tears; it is a gathering place. (Rudolf Steiner, *Kosmogonie*)[8]

For some individuals, the sexual force can be a very strong and active potency within the will. When the individuality's capacity to individualize the will forces is suppressed, it can cause the sexual forces that also live in the will to be diverted in negative ways. One of the pictures from spiritual work that Rudolf Steiner gives is that if people don't allow the child's will to unfold healthily out of what they are here to bring in the form of deep interest in the world around them, then at puberty, when the instinctual sexual forces are awakening, these can be more easily diverted into two potential directions: the love of having power over others, and eroticism (focus on self-gratification and objectification).[9] Although this is expressed in the will sphere, it also affects the feeling and thinking of the person.

What is it that I'm here to bring through my will? This is something we each have to understand for ourselves. If it is not able to unfold in the way that it truly intends to, then our will can unfold in a way colored by one diversion, or the other, and often by both. We can see that the domination of one will over another will, as well as eroticism for the sake of self-gratification, go hand-in-hand in much of what has become the commonly held picture of so-called normal sexuality.

When we look at these two spheres—eroticism and love of power—then we may say, "That's not me, I don't stand on that ground in my life." But what is eroticism? In its simplest sense, it is when I want to gratify myself sensually—whereas, in the opposite pole, I want to dominate the other. And those two feelings—that of gratifying myself, gratifying my sensory being so that I delight in self-stimulation, leading to my self-satisfaction, and that of dominating the other—these are both a part of us all as a potential possibility, to some degree, in the realm of our will impulses. The self-gratification aspect of this potential within each human will nature reveals itself in the various phases of the pathway to addiction. Our love of power is also a common trait in the everyday will—it is one of the aspects of the human "shadow," or lower nature, to want to raise ourselves above others: to experience power, the diminishing of another—to want to get ahead even at the expense of another human being.

When the imbalance is operating in our feeling life, then we generally experience its expression in two ways: one is shame and the other is anxiety. The mental health organization in Australia recently published a report that one in four Australian children say they are anxious or worried most or all of the time. Why is mental health becoming the greatest concern for teenagers? The feeling of shame is often expressed by them as "not being good enough," which can include feeling ashamed about their body image. With the experience of shame comes the wish to disappear, to blend in, to not be seen. Characterized physiologically, the blood moves to the periphery of the body; the face flushes as we try to dissolve ourselves into the environment. The opposite effect takes place with anxiety: the face becomes pale, we contract away from the world, and we build a fortress within ourselves, trying to control the impact of the outer world by maintaining an inner defense. Disappearing and defending are common gestures among young people.

In the thinking capacity, this imbalance shows itself in the quality of being judgmental and opinionated—or, in the opposite way, as a merely associative thinking faculty. When we are judging the other, we do not let the other in; we do not experience the world from their point of view. We block the other through our judgments, criticizing them and opposing them. In associative thinking, we relate everything to ourselves; everything that is said or revealed to us is related to the past of what we ourselves have already experienced. We let the thoughts of others in, but then blend their thoughts into what we already know; we make the new thought confirm or validate the thoughts we already carry.

All of these diversions in the thinking, feeling, or will lead the individual toward becoming a *persona*, a caricature of itself in the personality. They lead one to become a person who is unable to experience true intimacy with the world, or on the other hand, become like an automaton—not thinking, feeling, or acting out of themselves, but out of the "script" of prior conditioning.

When human beings are not allowed to bring their individual spiritual capacities to expression fully into the world, the results are some form of diversion of their fundamental creative force, in a distracting or even destructive manner, onto the other or themselves. These diversions will come to expression in the creative forces of the will, the feeling life, or the thinking life—and usually they are expressed to some degree in all three.

We each have to contend with our inner life being continuously influenced by the collective consciousness of the community. The forces in us that are diverted through the errors of the not-yet-progressive aspects of the collective consciousness leave marks upon us in childhood, and continue to affect us in our daily life as adults. Due to these outer influences and hindrances, we often become disturbed in our ability to rightly perceive others and ourselves; these disturbances can be balanced and harmonized through certain inner exercises.

The primary way to combat such outer hindrances and restore or develop them into healthy capacities requires that we create renewed inner conditions for ourselves through exercises that bring about a harmonizing and strengthening of the soul life. Such exercises are given in slightly different ways in various schools for inner development. They are presented in what follows according to what has been given by Rudolf Steiner in the form of the "six subsidiary exercises" described in his books *How to Know Higher Worlds* and *An Outline of Esoteric Science,* as well as in the compilation *Guidance in Esoteric Training,* which is quoted at length in the next several pages.[10]

> The first condition is the cultivation of absolutely clear thinking.
> The second condition is the control of will.
> The third condition is the control of feeling.
> The fourth condition is the cultivation of a "positive attitude."
> The fifth condition is to develop the feeling of confronting every new experience with complete open-mindedness.
> The sixth condition is to gradually develop a beautiful equilibrium of soul.

We begin with the first condition—control of thinking—for one month, adding to this exercise the second condition in the second month, then the third condition in the third month, and so forth. It is useful to add the next exercise even if you have not succeeded in the month before, as the power gained from the new exercise may be the very thing you needed to manage the previous one more successfully.

The First Condition: Cultivation of Clear Thinking

For this exercise, pupils must rid themselves of will-o'-the-wisp thought, even if only for a very short time during the day. About five minutes is enough, but the longer the better.

Pupils must become the ruler of their own world of thought. We are not the ruler if the way we think is determined by external circumstances, one's occupation, some tradition or other, social relationships, membership in a particular race, the daily round of life, certain activities, and so forth.

Therefore, during this brief time—acting entirely out of our own free will—we must empty the soul of the ordinary, everyday flow of thoughts, and by our own initiative place one single thought at the center of our soul.

The thought need not be a particularly striking or interesting one. Indeed, it will be even better for what has to be attained in an esoteric sense if a thoroughly uninteresting and insignificant thought is chosen. Our thinking capacity is then prompted to act out of its own energy, which is the essential thing here; in contrast, an interesting thought has the effect of carrying the thinking along with it.

It is better if this exercise in thought control is undertaken with a pin rather than with Napoleon. The pupil says to him- or herself: I will start from this thought, and through my own inner initiative I will associate with it everything that is pertinent to it. At the end of the period of the exercise, the thought should be just as colorful and living as it was at the beginning. This exercise is repeated from one day to the next for at least a month; a new thought may be taken every day, or the same thought may be adhered to for several days.

At the end of the exercise, an endeavor is made to become fully conscious of the inner feeling of firmness and security that will soon be noticed by paying subtler attention to one's own soul. The exercise is then brought to a conclusion by focusing the thinking upon the head and the middle of the spine (brain and spinal cord), as if the feeling of security were being poured into this part of the body.

These exercises are practiced with the aim of developing a mastery over our own inner life, freeing it, as it were, for a receptive attitude toward the influences of the outer world. Therefore, it is not a matter of striving to know everything about the object that we choose as our focus. It is not a matter of outwardly investigating it, but rather of concentrating our thinking on the chosen object. Again, it is more fruitful if one is not outwardly looking at the chosen object, but rather picturing it within your mind's eye. "Practice this exercise for approximately one month, and then add the second requirement."

The Second Condition: Control of the Will

We try to think of some action that, in the ordinary course of life, we will certainly not have performed. Then, we make it a duty to perform this action every day. It will therefore be good to choose an action that can be performed every day, and that one can continue to perform for as long a period of time as possible.

Again, it is better to begin with some insignificant action that we will have to force ourselves to perform—for example, to water a flower we have bought at a fixed time every day. After a certain period of time, a second similar action should be added to the first—later a third, and so on...as many as are compatible with the carrying out of all our other duties.

This exercise should likewise last for one month. But as far as possible, the first exercise should also continue alongside the second during this second month, although it will become a less dominant duty than it was during the first month. Nevertheless, the first month's practice must not be left unheeded, for otherwise it will quickly be noticed that the fruits of the first month are lost and the slovenliness of uncontrolled thinking begins again. Care must be taken that once these fruits have been won, they are never again lost.

If, through the second exercise, this quality of "initiative of action" has been achieved, then, with subtle attentiveness, we become conscious of the feeling of an inner impulse of activity in the soul. We pour this feeling/experience into the body, letting it stream from the head down into and around the heart.

Although many people struggle with this exercise, it is important to realize that each exercise is in fact quite challenging: the great effort required of us is the very means whereby these exercises serve to develop inner strength, and even to provide inner control and self-reliance to those who are dedicated enough in their practice. The will exercise seems particularly difficult, and that is because only with the will exercise can we immediately see whether or not the goal has been achieved. It may be that we are just as poor in the attention needed for the thinking exercise as we are in that needed for the will exercise, but that we do not perceive our lack of thinking–attentiveness as clearly as we can perceive the task left undone.

The Third Condition: Control of Feeling

In the third month, life should be centered on a new exercise: the development of a certain equanimity toward the fluctuations of joy and sorrow, pleasure and pain. The "heights of jubilation" and "depths of despair" should quite consciously be replaced by an equable mood. Care should be taken that no pleasure will carry us away, no sorrow plunge us into the depths, no experience lead to immoderate anger or irritation, no expectation give rise to anxiety or fear, no situation disconcert us, and so on.

There need be no fear that such an exercise will make life barren and unproductive; rather, it will quickly be noticed that the experiences to which this exercise is applied are replaced by purer qualities of soul. Above all, if subtle attentiveness is maintained, an inner tranquility in the body will one day become noticeable. As in the two cases above, we should now pour this feeling into the body, letting it stream from the heart toward the hands, the feet, and finally the head.

This naturally cannot be done after each period of practicing this exercise—for here it is not primarily a matter of one single exercise, but of sustained attentiveness to the inner life of the soul. However, at least once every day, this inner tranquility should be called up before the soul and should be followed by the practice of "pouring out" from the heart what has been inwardly cultivated through the exercise.

A connection with the exercise of the previous months should once again be maintained, as was done during the second month with regard to the exercise of the first month.

Inner objectivity is gained to a heightened degree through the "control of feeling" exercise. Even as feelings well up, we maintain an ability to witness them rather than identify ourselves with them. There may then grow within us a capacity to calm the waters of feeling turbulence at will. As one continues with this practice, one will not experience that the feelings have grown dull at all, but rather that one can master their expression if need be. At the very least, one will be able to witness the feelings and choose whether or not to act them out.

The Fourth Condition: Cultivation of a Positive Attitude

In the fourth month, as a new exercise, what is sometimes called a "positive attitude to life" should be cultivated. It consists in seeking always for the good, the praiseworthy, the beautiful, and the like, in all beings, all experiences, and all things.

This quality of soul is best characterized by a Persian legend concerning Christ Jesus, which Rudolf Steiner recounted in this connection. One day, as Christ Jesus was walking with His disciples, they saw a dead dog lying by the roadside in a state of advanced decomposition. All the disciples turned away from the disgusting sight; Christ Jesus alone did not move, but looked thoughtfully at the corpse and said: "What beautiful teeth the animal has!" Where the others had seen only the repulsive, the unpleasant, He looked for the beautiful.

So must the esoteric pupil strive to seek for the positive in every phenomenon and in every being. The pupil will soon notice that under the veil of something repugnant, there is a hidden beauty—that even under the outer guise of a criminal, there is a hidden good—that under the mask of a lunatic, the divine soul is somehow concealed.

In a certain respect, this exercise is connected with what is called "abstention from criticism" (nonparticipation in criticism). This is not to be understood in the sense of calling black white and white black. There is, however, a difference between a judgment that, proceeding merely from one's own personality, is colored with the element of personal sympathy or antipathy, and an attitude that enters lovingly into the alien phenomenon or being, always asking: How has it come to be like this or to act like this? Such an attitude will, by its very nature, be more set upon helping what is imperfect than upon simply finding fault and criticizing.

The argument that the very circumstances of their lives oblige many people to find fault and condemn is not valid here. For in such cases, the circumstances are such that the person in question cannot go through a genuine esoteric training.

If it has once been noticed that the feeling described expresses itself in the soul as a kind of bliss, then endeavors should be made in thought to guide this feeling/experience into the heart, and from there to let it stream into the eyes, and onward out into the space in front of and around oneself. It will be noticed that an intimate relationship to this surrounding space is thereby acquired. Pupils grow out of and beyond themselves, as it were. Pupils learn to regard a part of their environment as something that belongs to them.

A great deal of concentration is necessary for this exercise, and above all, recognition of the fact that all unrestrained feelings, all passions, and all overly exuberant emotions have an absolutely destructive effect upon the mood indicated.

The exercises of the earlier months are also to be repeated, as was done before.

As with the previous exercises, the positivity exercise has effects reaching much further than merely how we meet

day-to-day circumstances. Positivity is a necessity in deal-
ing with all aspects of the inner path of evolution. Without
it, we would give up, turn back, or feel overwhelmed by the
mountain of obstacles that face us in our task of genuine
transformation. Positivity is the sign that the student of the
inner work is becoming stronger against outer hindrances.

The Fifth Condition: Develop a Feeling of Confronting Every New Experience with Complete Open-mindedness

In the fifth month, efforts should be made to develop the
feeling of confronting every new experience without any
prejudgments. The esoteric student must break entirely
with the attitude that, in the face of something just heard
or seen, exclaims: "I've never heard or seen that before; I
don't believe it—it's an illusion."

At every moment, the pupil must be ready to
encounter and accept absolutely new experiences.
What the pupil previously recognized as being in
accordance with natural law, or what they regarded
as possible, should present no obstacle to the acceptance of a new truth. Although radically expressed, it
is absolutely correct that if anyone were to come to the
esoteric pupil and say, "Since last night, the steeple of
such and such a church has been tilted right over," the
pupil should leave a loophole open for the possibility
of becoming convinced that their previous knowledge
of natural law could somehow be increased by such an
apparently unprecedented fact.

Open-mindedness is not only necessary for inner strengthening—it is also the gesture that all students of inner schooling must cultivate in order to allow for other possibilities and
realities to be perceived. In this way, we are guarded from the

46

blunting effects of the material world and kept open to the enlivening effects of the Mysteries of life.

The Sixth Condition: The Gradual Development of a Beautiful Equilibrium of Soul

In the sixth month, endeavors should be made to repeat all five exercises again, systematically and in regular alternation. In this way, a beautiful equilibrium of soul will gradually develop. It will especially be noticed that previous dissatisfactions with certain phenomena and beings in the world completely disappear.

A mood of "reconciling all experiences" now gradually takes hold of the soul—a mood that is by no means one of indifference, but, on the contrary, a mood that enables one for the first time to work in the world for the sake of the world's genuine progress and improvement. One comes to a tranquil understanding of things that were formerly quite closed to the soul.

These exercises can be taken on by all individuals wanting to strengthen themselves against the outer hindrances of the world, as well as to come into stronger connection with the forms of outer support that the world provides. The many erroneous thoughts, feelings, and impulses of the collective consciousness will no longer have the same influence upon us, and the beneficial and progressive elements of the collective consciousness will emerge more clearly into the forefront. Through carrying out these exercises, we will not feel the great burden of the collective consciousness; but instead, greater hope in human progress will awaken within us. Along with this hope will arise a greater will to participate in positive change for the world.

2

THE DEVELOPING COMPLEXITY
OF ATTRACTION

The human being, as we understand it through the light of spiritual reality, does not merely consist of a physical–material body. In all traditions, there is an understanding that there also exists the human soul life or consciousness, which is not to be identified with the body. While many of these various schools of thought are in general agreement as to the many aspects of the human being, some try to further assess and distinguish the various components as a way of understanding the complexity of being human and our relationship to both the physical and spiritual worlds.

Many schools of spiritual thought, especially the esoteric ones, work to define the human being in terms of the various sheaths or bodies to understand the dimensions of experience we can have, both in the physical world and beyond the physical–material realm. These groups often use different terminology, and some may have limited expressions as compared with others, but all try to understand the human being and its relationship to the surrounding world in order to help perceive and share what is beyond the sense perceptible.

> When we consider what grows over and beyond the differences of gender, we see the higher nature of the human

being—what the "I" creates out of the lower bodies. Man and woman must look upon their physical body as a vehicle that enables them, in one direction or another, to be active as a totality in the physical world. The more human beings become aware of the spiritual within them, the more does the body become an instrument, and the more do they come to understand the nature of the human being by seeing into the depths of the soul. (Rudolf Steiner, "Women and Society")[11]

Unlike the natural sciences, which seek to weigh and measure the sense-perceptible world through external instruments, those endeavoring to enquire beyond the material world must additionally use the instrument of their own soul being in order to perceive the soul–spiritual dimensions. This endeavor was termed *spiritual science* by Rudolf Steiner.

Even if we are not ourselves a spiritual scientist or a natural scientist, there is a capacity for common sense and healthy human understanding that we all carry within us. Even though useful expressions of insight are often given by other people, with effort we can still follow the thinking of others and the meaning of their thoughts, because we have some degree of direct knowing of these things through our individual life experiences.

Solid substance, shape, and form exist in minerals, plants, animals, and human beings in the form of the physical sheath. This is the body that we see and perceive, and that relates us to the sense-perceptible world. It gives a human being shape and form, and through it we are able to perceive the human being in space. It can be weighed, measured, dissected, and analyzed by all the instruments of the natural scientist.

Life, growth, the maintaining of life, dying, and death belong to the plant world, the animal world, and to human beings. We are not just members of the physical–mineral realm; we also possess a life body. Through the forces of this life body, the cells draw the strength to repair and develop themselves. The growth of the body and the maintenance of this growth are all dependent on the body of life processes. This life body is also connected to our external existence and our life on earth, but it is unseen except for the results of its activity as they come to expression in the external, physical body. The life body is still being explored and is not yet understood by the natural scientist.

However, we also extend beyond the plant kingdom by virtue of the fact that we have a sentient body. Unlike the minerals and the plants, the human being and the animal can also experience and respond to the world around them through the nerve and sensory system. This sensitivity system allows us to experience pleasure and pain. It gives sensation inwardly and it responds to the stimuli that it takes in from the world. It also allows us to have inner responses such as hunger and feelings of wellness and unwellness. This complex sensitivity system in the human being is observable and detectable by the natural sciences primarily through the brain, which functions as its center. However, the human being's inner experiences extend beyond the aspects of the sensitivity system that can be physically observed and measured. It extends beyond these insofar as we also experience ourselves as having an inner life. The scientifically observable imprints or effects in the brain are not the cause of the inner life—rather, they are the tracks or footprints laid down by the inner life.

We could say that the animal kingdom also has an inner life of this nature, since the animals, too, can feel and respond. But the human being's inner life takes us far beyond mere experience and response, for in the case of the human being we can also think independently, feel, and will our lives in an individual manner. It is this independent activity that "lays its tracks," and these tracks are then perceivable in the brain. This independent activity does not arise out of the brain. It is in these inner dimensions that we begin to recognize the soul–spiritual realities of human life. We alone, among all the kingdoms of nature, are able to change and transform the world around us in a self-willed way.

What gives us this capacity to change what is around us? What gives us this capacity for transformation? It is not what we have in common with the mineral kingdom (our physical sheath), nor is it what we have in common with the plant kingdom (our life body); not even our sentient body—what we have in common with the animal kingdom—allows for such capacities of change. What gives us the capacities for change and transformation that the other kingdoms do not have is the fact that the human being extends beyond the other kingdoms of our external world and has a different quality of inner life.

Human beings have an individuality, and this individuality is an expression of uniqueness, giving rise to our individual self-consciousness. As human beings, we are self-conscious beings. We express this self-consciousness with two little words, "I am." These two words raise the human being from the status of an animal to that of a self-aware and creative spiritual being.

> Those who judge human beings according to generic characteristics stop before the boundary beyond which people begin to be beings whose activity is based on free self-determination. What lies short of that boundary can, of course, be an object of scientific investigation. Racial, tribal, national, and sexual characteristics form the content of specific sciences. Only persons who want to live merely as examples of a genus can fit themselves into a generic picture derived from such scientific investigation. But all these sciences together cannot penetrate to the specific content of single individuals. Where the region of freedom (in thinking and action) begins, determination of individuals by the laws of the genus comes to an end.... People can be considered free spirits within the human community only to the degree that they free themselves from the generic in this way. (Rudolf Steiner, *Intuitive Thinking as a Spiritual Path: A Philosophy of Freedom*)[12]

This spiritual part of the human being individuates our lives into unique expressions—and yet, at the same time, it is the greatest unifying factor among human beings. As human beings, we all have the "I am," and yet only as individuals can we each say "I am" to ourselves. This self-consciousness is expressed also in our capacity to be present, attentive, and purposefully directed in our engagement with the world around us. Through the "I," individuals are able to take hold of their inner life; and through the capacities of thinking, feeling, and willing, we are able to make changes in the world around us. Through the "I," we are individuals and can become individually creative beings.

The capacities of thinking, reasoning, learning, and understanding awaken us to very important aspects of being human. We are thinking beings, and through our capacity to think, reason, and learn, we are likewise growing and developing.

If we consider the animal kingdom and observe how a particular species has grown and developed over the last thousand years, we will perceive very few changes to the behavior or way of life of that species.

And yet, if we consider the development of the human being over the last thousand years, we can see immense changes in many spheres of human existence. We have changed in both our outer and inner life. From our lifespan to our intellectual capacity and how it comes to expression, we have changed dramatically. There have also been major changes in what we call "community life" and how we live together: from where we live in the world to how community life runs its daily course, so much change has taken place for the human being.

We cannot look at the various animal species in this same way. The changes that have taken place in the animal kingdom have come about through its relationship to humankind.

It is not only through our thinking life that we are able to individualize ourselves, but we also experience the world in an individual way through feeling it—through our feelings, we allow the world in. Not only do we think and reason within the enclosure of our inner world; we also experience the outer world, and through our experiences we are informed by the world.

When we see a rose, we can also have an inner experience of this "outer thing" in our inner world—not only by association, but through the direct influence that our experience of the "outer thing" has on us. This inner movement, which brings about inner change and learning, is the outer world having an effect within us. This effect can take place in that initial moment of perception, but it can also be recalled again in our capacity for memory.

Think for a moment of a friend's smiling face; even though our friend is not present, through recollection we can still have an inner experience that moves us. In the moment of perception, or in the later recollection via memory of what we've earlier perceived, we can feel that our experience affects our inner life. What would human beings amount to if we were unable to let the world in and allow it to affect our individual inner experience?

A human being also has a capacity for volition, for will activity. We can do things that we choose to do; unlike the lion, we can decide to change our diet and become a vegetarian. Even if we have been brought up in a particular way culturally, socially, or religiously, we can still make a decision to change those things—to change how we act and what we do.

Unless an animal species has come into contact with the human being's will, generally the animal will not change things in its way of life of its own accord. Regardless of our conditioning, we recognize that we have an individual will. Whether we choose to utilize it or not, the human being has the capacity to will an individual life.

What is this individual capacity, this part of the human being that can direct our attention to thinking certain things, to recalling what we choose to recall, to focusing on aspects of the world in order to allow them to be experienced within us, to individually willing the kind of life that we wish to live?

The various aspects of the fourfold human constitution are in consistent relationship with one another within ourselves and within the world around us. This interpenetration between the four sheaths of the human being is what allows us to become aware of our individual selves, and it is what brings us into relationship with others. What attracts us to another can arise from one or more sheaths at a time. Experiencing an attraction to another human being is for many individuals a complex matter.

The fact that we have various different members or sheaths within our human organization gives rise to attractions arising from different places within us. Although we may not have distinguished all the various levels of attraction, we are all aware of the complexity of the forms of attraction that we may experience toward others and from others.

When we experience conflict between the various aspects of attraction within us, we become more acutely aware of the differences arising from the various places within. For some people, there is no conflict between the various aspects of themselves and their attraction to others. This often results in less confusion or questions around sexuality, love, and friendship. However, even without inner conflict between the various pulls within, natural attractions can sometimes be more complicated in cases wherein individuals have experienced certain relationship patterns being expressed either around them or toward them directly during their earlier developmental years. Knowledge of this can be useful when working to support others in their work to see where and why their attractions may have taken an unhealthy path.

Inevitably, as a young person is growing, there is always some degree of confusion and questions as the various qualities of attraction are awoken at different stages of their growth and development. Well before the development of puberty and sexual attraction, the child begins to experience a feeling of attraction to others arising in their consciousness. Various aspects of attraction to others begin to enter their consciousness. Children can have "crushes" long before they reach puberty. These crushes have nothing to do with sexual orientation or sexuality. They arise out of an awakening of interest and curiosity in another's individual being and how it expresses itself in the world.

When we allow this healthy and natural development in childhood without imposing adult sexuality upon it, this provides children with the freedom to develop deeper and healthier inner capacities. It allows them to have a richer inner world. It is also typical for children to have crushes on various friends and adults once the force of sexual attraction awakens with the physical foundation of hormonal changes, but this is still not necessarily an indication of sexual orientation.

When working with young people, it is always important to teach them things in an age-appropriate way. We must consider why and how we teach certain things to the growing child. Unlike other subjects that they will learn at school, when it comes to the subject of gender and sexuality, much of what the adults around them inwardly hold to be true has already passed to the children through how we speak to people and react to situations in their presence.

Our approach to teaching young people has already begun even before we have consciously entered the subject. Therefore, if we want to be conscious about what we are going to pass onto them, we need to become clear about what lives in us, even subconsciously, as it's going to affect what we are able to bring to them.

Life presents us with new reasons every day for why it is worth communicating with young people in a way that supports where they are and how they are growing up. For example, we can use all the opportunities that arise to convey care for the body, appropriate boundaries, and respect in the context of cultivating healthy relationships to others. These opportunities should be taken even when children are as young as kindergarten age and clearly not yet in need of the content of the first sex education lessons on puberty and bodily changes. But all good work in this direction sets a ground for deeper conversations later on. The young child may say something like, "Boys are naughty." This is an opportunity to correct their gender stereotyping in an age-appropriate way. We have to be very conscious about how we use language around the children in relation to matters of gender, as it's simply not true that all boys are naughty—but the child has already acquired that concept.

The primary caregivers have the greatest influence on the young developing child, but because we partake in the collective consciousness, we are all influenced by the collective thoughts and customs in the community around us. Even though individual families may have made true headway in terms of gender stereotypes and sexism, the small child is nevertheless impressed upon by what lives in the collective atmosphere of the larger community. We're all responsible for the education of the next generation.

Small children are unaware of their sex or supposed gender, though it is often the first thing the surrounding community knows about them—even before they are born. Is it a girl or a boy? They are conditioned from the moment they are born by how they are treated, and by how they "should be" according to the perspective of the outer world. But of themselves, they do not consciously understand the differences between body types until they grow more fully into their bodily awareness, around age five.

The child can reflect through imitation what it has learned before the age of five, stating, "I am a boy"—and the child can even say what that means in some way, stating, "Boys have a penis." However, their own revelation of different body parts comes between ages four and five when the toddler's belly flattens out and the forces of awareness descend into the metabolic system. It is very common at this age for them to be interested in their genitals; they may naturally hold onto their genitals when being read a story, or when dreaming away from the external play around them. Mostly, this is only the natural consciousness awakening to these body parts. It comes hand in hand with the so-called bottom language of talking "poos" and "wees"—the general process of waking up to body parts in the metabolic system. They then begin to enquire about others' body parts; this awakening interest can lead them to want to play the role of doctor with each other. It is not an indicator of sexuality if the child is seen to be "playing doctor" with a similarly aged child of one sex or another. It is rather an indicator of the awakening awareness of these parts of the body, and therefore it is a good time to more consciously reinforce the guidelines for healthy body boundaries to the individual children involved. Before this age, it is not a matter of conscious instruction, but rather general, implicit guidelines around personal boundaries.

The instructions at this age should not be about sexuality, but simply about raising social awareness of the antisocial behavior of involving themselves in their "own body world." The instruction need not have its focus on the genitals, but should rather be focused on social interaction. If a child is engrossed in any of his or her own body parts publicly from the age of four onward, it appears antisocial. It is also antisocial if someone is fixated on his or her nose while in public, but if we give our nose a little scratch it's natural. So it is with the genitals: if it itches, a little scratch should not cause embarrassment, as it's just another body part. However, all self-engrossing behavior, publicly, of any body part should be curbed by the age of four. The primary way of achieving this is by distraction. Putting other things in their hands is a method that works well—or, leading them into another activity as a way of bringing their focus back to what they should be doing at that time rather than what they shouldn't be doing in public.

However, it is also the case that young children will often "self-sooth" by means of masturbation, as a way of pulling away from the external world. This could be a sign of sensory overload or hypersensitivity in the sensory system. Therefore, it is essential to take a holistic look at what is happening in the life of the child who feels the need to masturbate. At this age, masturbation is not a matter of a sexual drive arising from the biology, but rather a sensual experience of self that removes children from what is happening around them in what is often an overly stimulating environment.

The way we approach their expressions of enquiry into their bodies is an essential aspect of the education we are giving them. Does our response give them a sense of the body as something natural and needing to be cared for, or as something shameful and wrong? The same goes for the way we treat their enquiry into the entire world of play. We can allow them natural exploration, or criticize their choices.

They are also aware, by ages four to five, of how they are being treated through the choices they make—for example, what clothes they can or cannot wear if they are a boy or a girl, or how they should or should not behave if they are a girl or a boy. Inevitably, by this age some children already feel that they do not fit into the so-called norm—they feel that they do not fit into the framework of the rules given to them. They already feel different from the collective way of life around them. They are being impressed upon by the collective consciousness from the moment of birth, but now they begin to become aware of the distinction between what is expected of them and what they prefer or don't prefer for themselves.

As the development of their consciousness descends into the metabolic system, it supports the separation between the self and the outer world. This duality is reflected in the inner experiences of "what is in me" versus "what is being asked of me." Around age five, awareness of the differences between what is outside and what is inside begins to awaken.

It is important for us to recognize as a community that gender stereotyping is prevalent everywhere. The children only have to open their mathematics book to see what the community thinks. Mathematics is a realm of study that has no functional use for the application of gender (unlike other realms, such as sports, where pitting male against female may cause a disadvantage owing to physical strength or other differences), and yet the mathematics book says to the young children, "Jack has twelve bricks; Lucy has six pink ribbons; Jack likes to play with bricks and build things; Lucy likes to put the ribbons in her dolly's hair." Already the young child may feel, "I'm not like how I should be." To the majority of growing young people, there comes a time when they recognize that what lives in them does not fit with the images continuously presented to them of how they should be. For some, this begins to become conscious at a young age—as young as at age five, the child may feel, "I am not the same as I should be." For others, it is not until greater unfolding of the various sheaths has occurred that they feel able to assess themselves in relationship to the wider beliefs held by the community. By the time they are adolescents, all young people feel some form of not fitting in or not having a place in today's society.

It is important that those giving classes in sex education in schools are particularly comfortable in meeting the topic of gender and sexuality. Educators must be sure not to express their own biases if they want to educate children and adolescents in a way that is supportive of their freedom. One's own bias—whether or not it happens to fall in line with the opinions of the majority of the community at the present time—will inevitably contribute to an experience of not fitting in for some students.

Conscious lessons in different aspects of sex education and gender education can rightfully be introduced at different stages of child development. To begin with, in the school setting, it is best for the class to consciously discuss puberty rather than sexuality itself.

The primary reason to speak with children about puberty in the school setting is that it helps to develop social understanding and ease in relation to the normal unfolding of their bodies. Therefore, even though not all children will enter puberty at the same age, it is still useful to bring to them the content of puberty once several members of the class have entered this phase. For this reason, we may need to bring in lessons about puberty to ten-year-olds, and continue to repeat and deepen these lessons each year. By age thirteen, all of the young people will naturally be at some stage of puberty, and then the school could include the more complex understanding of puberty leading into sexuality. These talks now need to include the various aspects of attraction and the inner complexity of being drawn to others, in order to meet the individual students where they are and to bring social consideration to what others in the class are experiencing.

Parents and guardians need to educate children about puberty in ways that meet them as individuals, because each child will enter puberty at different ages, and understanding puberty before entering it is a part of supporting their health. The parents or guardians of such children need to begin to express the natural pictures of puberty as a preparation for the children before they begin to show the outer signs of it.

In school, however, it is necessary to bring puberty to the class not on an individual basis, but on a social basis. The social aspect of the way we approach the changes in the body at puberty serves as a foundation for how we will treat each other in later phases of life. To see the transition from the small child through to the adult body as a natural process that is not connected to sexuality helps the child to recognize the rightful place of puberty. It is not about being ready for sex or sexuality, but rather about growing into an adult body. If we can deal with this in as natural and as social a way as possible, it will help us to develop respect and care between the members of the class. The care we put into our way of approaching this can come to have a very protective effect for children in later years. If the members of the younger classes can cultivate friendship and deep social understanding for each other—both for the similarities and for the differences— then when they reach the upper grades, they will tend to look out for each other instead of "acting out" the struggles of adolescence on each other.

In our time, healthy and effective sex education needs to be a social education that comes more from a place of health and wellbeing than is found in the traditional mechanics of biology and physiology. The process of social education begins with an understanding of the various bodily changes, inner experiences, and aspects of growth during puberty. A social approach to sex education and gender education is not a matter of replacing the formal sex education curriculum, but of attempting to make it healthier and more harmonious in the way it lives in the experience of the child or adolescent. And it is essential for us to recognize that they are already receiving an influential and mostly distorted form of "social sex- and gender-education" through social media.

We always aim to bring to children an understanding of what is socially required for them to understand the world and to be in a balanced relationship to others in the community. An understanding of puberty should be brought at an age during which it is useful for children, because it has already become a part of their social world.

Although a basic groundwork for this direct and explicit discussion of puberty around age ten would naturally have come about already in earlier years through social conversations and relationships to the world, it is still important that children feel they are being taught by someone who understands what they are experiencing. It's not that they need to be taught by someone who is academically qualified—and certainly not by those who are heavily engaged in the subject on an intellectual level—but by someone who can convey to them, through social ease, what they are going through and how natural it is.

When teaching about puberty as a bodily experience, it is important that we meet it in the most natural and human way in order that we can allow these images of change and transition to live harmoniously in the soul of the child.

There is also no need to make the biological changes happening in the body into a "special thing." Some people, rather than teaching from the intellectual, swing to the opposite pole and put far too much sentimental importance on these natural processes. The idea of expressing to children that "they are now a man or a woman" because they have entered puberty offers an erroneous picture in our present consciousness. Although it is a significant event in the body's transition process, puberty is not adulthood in the true sense. Having puberty ceremonies and dressing the children up in "puberty gowns" is really a sentimental approach that is not useful to the awakening "self-consciousness soul life" of the individual.

As adults, the organs that come to maturation during puberty are utilized very individually as an expression of each person's individual life. The fact is that, for many individuals, their sexual organs do not play a significant role in their adult life. Many individuals today choose not to have children—they do not use the genitalia as a form of procreation. For many individuals, the sexual organs become a form of pleasure and perhaps an expression of joy in the body. For others, the genitalia play a role of little importance in their life and are not utilized for sexual activity. We should not make the assumption that the way our genitalia have affected our own life will be the same for any other individual.

It is also erroneous to our present consciousness when adults divide the students into groups of boys and girls before talking about gender and sexuality. This does not reflect the scientific understanding of what is most supportive for true learning—nor does separating them reflect a spiritual understanding of our present task, which is to work with them in a way that focuses on their individual inner being. Separating them has a negative effect on the soul aspect of the education and on their feeling of place within the community. By its very nature, the act of separating children along the lines of outer sexual characteristics serves to place them within a framework of gender stereotypes that is fast becoming antiquated. This does not serve them in the task of developing the social understanding that is necessary to meet the new social forms emerging in our time.

In all of these areas, it is clear that the task of transforming the past requires new forms of education around sexuality and gender. In the early 1900s, Rudolf Steiner described how far we have yet to come in this domain—and although we have made numerous advances, it still acts as a distorting influence when we rear children in a one-sided manner according to their outer characteristics.

> Keep in mind that the boys and girls are always taught together in the Waldorf School, right up to the highest class.... This has a social effect as well—mutual understanding between the sexes, which is tremendously important today. We still tend to be very unsocial and

prejudiced in this matter. (Rudolf Steiner, *The Spiritual Ground of Education*)[13]

It is helpful and necessary to teach children about physiological puberty with all gender groups together so that they can gain both an understanding of themselves as well as a social understanding for others. One of the methods by which this can be brought in a natural way is to show children how they previously moved through a cycle of development in the transition of the change of teeth.

Bringing the example of the change of teeth is a great way to prepare the ten- or eleven-year-old child to understand that normal and necessary changes will be taking place within them and their peers, and that they have already gone through a similar cycle once before as the body grew from a small to a grown child.

In the class setting, the educator may ask the children if they can remember the age when they lost their first tooth. Not all will remember, but many do. Some say four, some five, many say six, and some say seven or eight. The educator then talks about how they have continued to lose their teeth from that starting age on—that in the transition from a small child's body to a grown child's body, everyone needs to go through the ongoing process of the change of teeth. But losing teeth and going through this change is not the same for everyone; some lose several teeth at once, whereas others lose one or two at regular intervals—and some lose teeth here and there.

Some people like losing teeth; they can even enjoy wiggling their loose tooth. Others find it difficult and even want to avoid eating hard things in case it affects their teeth, while still others find it uncomfortable until they gradually get used to it. Our relationship to this change varies from one individual to another. But basically, to get from the condition of a small child's body into that of a grown child's body, all of us must undergo the necessity of changing our first teeth in order to acquire our adult teeth. From the first lost tooth right through to the loss of the twelve-year-old molars, there are many years of transition until they have what are known as the full set of "adult teeth." It is not as if children wake up one morning to find their mouth full of adult teeth. Rather, even though they are not yet adults, slowly, over time they acquire the teeth that they will have for the rest of their lives.

An understanding of this process sets the ground for connecting the change of teeth with the young person's experience of puberty. Like the change of teeth, the first signs of puberty will come naturally at different ages. Puberty is just another phase of growth through which the physical body is shifting from a child's body toward an adult body.

The most common age range for the first clear signs of the onset of bodily puberty is from nine to thirteen years old. But here, again, the process doesn't happen overnight; just as we don't wake up one morning with a full set of new adult teeth, so puberty does not mean that children are going to wake up one morning as a "big person." As with the change of teeth, the signs and stages of puberty occur over an extended period of time.

With the ten, eleven, and twelve-year-olds, rather than teaching them about puberty, it is most useful to ask them to describe the signs of puberty. What are the changes that the body goes through during puberty? By asking the children what they know, this gives a clear indication of how the pictures of puberty are living in them. It also gives the educator the opportunity to harmonize and bring healing to the pictures that the students are already carrying. It is an opportunity to dispel the myths that leave hindering impressions within them as individuals as well as between them as peers.

In general, it is best for the educator to respond to the pictures of puberty that are already known by the children at the age of ten to eleven, not adding entirely new content to what the group knows, but rather taking what they know and expanding and integrating it. For instance, a ten-year-old will recognize that there are bodily changes during puberty. It is common for them to say something like "Girls get big boobs." That one simple point expressed by the child can be developed into a thought that harmonizes with a true understanding of him- or herself and others.

The response may be something like this: "Yes, if you have a predominantly female body, then you're very likely to get some changes in the breast tissue. But what you might not know is that this can also happen quite naturally if you have a predominantly male body." This is a way of talking about how the body goes through various shifts as it is growing and changing, before finally settling into a defined shape and form.

This point brought up by the child can now be extended— for example, by saying that we have no choice over our breast size, as it is a part of our physiology and heredity. This may then extend to talking about testicle and penis size, and how the testicles and penis are also growing—but that this is not as obvious to the outside world as breast growth is. This can be an opportunity to talk about the respect and kindness we need to show each other while going through the transition of puberty—that all of us will go through this transition, but that it can be more difficult for some as their body goes through big changes. The educator may also speak about body image and how it is affecting people's wellbeing. Extending the picture of body image, we might now talk about how the young person's consciousness has changed from the way it was when they were little. We can remind them how easy it was in kindergarten to not worry about what other people thought of them, of how they dressed or what they looked like—but how now, as they grow up, they become more aware of these things. It is now a good opportunity to mention the three soul experiences (described in chapter 1), which at some point will unfold within them, as well as explaining how even now some children of their age are beginning to fear rejection and look for acceptance from the group. Also, how all the children can begin to feel longing, as if something is missing in their lives or that they are missing out on something. It can also be mentioned that, at this age, we can at times begin to feel lonely, isolated, or more separated from others.

Every aspect that the children already know about puberty is an opportunity for us to help them to better understand themselves and the other. Each year, they tend to know a little more.

By the age of twelve, all the aspects of puberty that the class has not brought forward out of themselves are now filled in. For instance, not too many children aged ten will speak about sexual urges or menstruation as a sign of puberty, but they will readily speak about more externalized changes such as body shape, breast growth, hair growth, changes in body odor and changes in emotions. By the age of twelve, it is useful for them to have a fuller picture of the effects of puberty and how they vary from individual to individual.

With groups of children around age thirteen, we can bring their attention to the fact that most in the class could biologically be parents—and yet, how many thirteen-year-olds are actually ready to be parents? Here we see the clear difference between biological readiness and the inner maturity necessary to manage all the things that can come along with sexual activity or love relationships with others.

Further, this fact begins to show students the distinction between biological processes and what takes place in the human soul life. It begins to reveal the fact that the vehicle in which we live cannot be the determining force of our life's path. If that were the case, we would be inclined to act like other mammals in the animal kingdom, simply reproducing from the moment the body is able to.

Taking this picture further into the experience of teenagers, we can begin to differentiate which forces of attraction within us arise out of our biology, and which forces arise out of our individuality and our humanness. What form of attraction differentiates us from the animal kingdom and makes us human?

With thirteen-year-olds, we can begin to explore these questions from a social point of view. What attracts us to others? Or what is it that, socially, we are told is attractive? By asking these questions, the educator has a chance to see the effects of social media on this age group, and can then support the harmonizing of this one-sidedness.

We then write a list of all the things that are seen as attractive on the board, and ask the question: Does this arise from biology? If so, then we would see it in some form in the animal kingdom as well.

So, for example, someone might say that big breasts or well-defined abs are attractive qualities. And although we could not say that an animal chooses its partner based on these particular things, we do know that in certain groups of animals, the visible procreative capacity of the other determines "mate-ability."

In the animal kingdom, for instance, stags will fight to determine strength, and then the strongest stag will mate with more doe in order to reproduce stronger offspring. The dog with the most power gets more food and more sex. It is very interesting to observe how much of what is held to be attractive in mass social media can be found expressed somewhere in the animal kingdom.

It is quiet extraordinary for young people to do this exercise together, because through the social media they generally do not become aware of these conditions, as they're so bombarded with external images of what is supposed to be attractive. But they also know there is much more happening than merely external attraction. It is often a relief for them to hear their own classmates saying that what they find attractive are qualities other than external looks. These are often things like similar humor—if the other makes them laugh. Also, the individual's personality, whether they are kind, whether they are considerate. These observations begin to show themselves in the class. They gradually express a type of attractiveness based on having things in common. In that they find others attractive who like similar things or have similar interests, the young people express their experience of attractiveness in ways that only belong to being human.

Going by what we find in the mass social media, the qualities held to be "attractive" primarily come down to looks, power, fame, and money. The young people themselves quickly recognize how relatively unimportant these qualities are in comparison to the more human qualities of attraction.

It is in this conversation that we can really begin to look at the social conditioning that takes us away from the most deeply important aspects of our human connections.

It is also an opportunity to look at the social conditioning found in different cultures regarding definitions of attractiveness and expected behaviors, according to whether one is born male or female. For example, young men in India are culturally more affectionate in public, regardless of their sexual orientation; they hold hands publicly, they stroke each other's chests publicly, they walk arm in arm down the street.

We can also look at what is socially held to be attractive in certain cultures and yet is in the process of changing through the influences of other cultures. We can see that, depending on where people are born in the world, they will be largely under the influence of that particular social conditioning.

This does not just come down to how we look physically, but also to what we can do in that culture and what we can wear in that culture. When we look into different cultures and the expectations placed upon individual men and women within those cultures, we begin to see just how much social conditioning affects what we come to see as genuinely acceptable if one is a man or a woman.

We can also look back in history in order to see the changes that have taken place. For instance, it wasn't long ago that you could not commonly wear pants if you were a woman. And it was even more recently that you could not be a stay-at-home parent if you were a man.

For both men and women, our options were more limited only a short time ago. And although it seems strange for female students now, the reality was that if you were born in a female body in the West and wanted to work, you were limited in your career choices to being a teacher, a secretary, or a nurse.

What is recognized by the students through these conversations is the ever-changing progress of society around the topic of gender, as well as the realization that depending on where a person was born, they would be educated in different ways, as well as be either more or less free in the amount of choices they have for how to live their lives. The students can also come to see the continual limitations placed upon them by the mass media—especially around body image and the over-sexualization even of young people. They see how the media has normalized the sexualization of young people, making many of them feel that this kind of attention from others is what should be cultivated in order to be normal.

At this young age, it is more useful to young people that they deeply understand the maturation process than it is that they understand the mechanics of the body. We have already touched on the emotional changes that take place, which can be explained during the "puberty talks"—but bringing even deeper levels of understanding to sex education helps the young people to navigate the more difficult aspects of puberty. It seems to have become a necessity in our time that in the school setting, we are also called upon to bring social understanding as a part of the curriculum. However, it would be useful to bring some of this within the home life in a natural way, earlier than when the students encounter it in school life. We need to consider that the education the young ones are receiving from their relationships with peers and with social media is primarily one based on externalized images or pornography. Therefore, it is our job to give the other point of view.

The sexual world expressed to the young people by their peers and by social media is often confusing, disturbing, or both. The health-giving pictures of natural development would help them to feel at ease with the changes they are experiencing and perceiving in and around them. But these pictures would also help to fill in the essential realization that sexual relationships are not purely a biological impulse for human beings. This is important in many ways; much confusion arises when children think that all the experiences of attraction that arise within them mean the same thing.

At home, we also need to educate them about the complexity of human relationships, and why we do what we do in the different relationships in our lives. If a child asks, "When did you lose your virginity?" and if she or he is at an age when it's useful for you to answer explicitly, then this offers an opportunity to express the complexity of such an experience. Rather than saying, "I was such and such an age," it's beneficial to elaborate on the more human story of the event. Tell them about how you felt leading up to it, what was going on inside of you during the time leading up to that decision, giving a picture of all the complexities of our humanness. It needs to be true and full and bringing to expression how this decision has affected us, as well as what we may wish to have been different now that we are older and looking back on the event. Rather than focusing on the one event of the sexual act, we should try to bring it as a whole picture of human experience, including the dimensions of our being that become active and engaged in all our relationships to others.

We can begin to clarify the different aspects of attraction to fourteen-year-olds, as it is already becoming their experience. This can then be deepened and clarified for the fifteen-, sixteen-, and seventeen-year-olds, adding more layers of understanding at each age as their capacity to understand and interact with the content matures. For young people, the more we are able to provide a sex education that meets their experiences and helps them to make sense of these experiences, the more useful it is for them and their understanding of their peers.

It is important to ensure that we speak to young people of the multifaceted nature of attraction, rather than allowing them to think that attraction is only a matter of the sexual impulse, and that therefore the sexual act is all that needs to be talked about. In a social approach to sex education and gender education, it is unlikely that we would need to bring consciousness to the social aspect of the sexual act until the majority of the class is sixteen years of age.

It's not really until we reach adulthood that we can begin to distinguish, with deep clarity, the levels of attraction that show themselves within us. Even after adulthood, some individuals may still feel the fluidity of the four sheaths' various attractions, and therefore not choose to fix themselves into certain categories of sexual orientation or romantic love; whereas for others, they may feel more certain in their orientation, even though it is still possible that this will change for them later in life. Therefore it can take time for every individual to identify their own sexual orientation because of the complexity of the interaction between the various sheaths within us.

We can observe the different ways that people in our time are trying to give expression to these various experiences arising within them. People may describe themselves as bisexual but "hetero–romantic," meaning that they are sexually attracted to both men and women but fall in love only with people of the opposite sex. Others might describe themselves as "pan-sexual," meaning they can feel sexually attracted to, and potentially open to, sexual encounters or relationships with individuals regardless of gender identity or sexual orientation. These terms are arising out of the popular culture, and they are continually changing. We are not trying to give the adolescents lessons in popular culture, but rather deeper insight into what they are seeing and experiencing, regardless of the term being used. Many of them feel that the terms or labels themselves are limiting. Our main task is to support their freedom, and merely following popular culture is not supportive of freedom. However, giving young people the tools to understand and evaluate what emerges in the popular culture and within themselves can support their freedom.

In the physical sheath, we can find the ground for our biologically based attraction. At our current stage of human development, most bodies show a certain single-sexed nature; therefore, in most individuals, the physical sheath has a tendency to be more male or more female. Although as science develops and as we are socially able to understand each other ever more deeply, we recognize that there is a greater spectrum of "maleness and femaleness," reaching even into the very biological, genetic, and hormonal profile that each individual carries.

Our varying degrees of "maleness or femaleness" in the physical sheath do not of themselves serve to explain our "chemistry" with another individual. Being born more male or more female in the physical sheath will not determine who we feel sexual chemistry with. We can partially understand this sexual chemistry rooted in our biology in terms of hormones and pheromones. Biological processes play a strong role in physical sexual attraction, along with our genetic profile. From both an anthropological and biological point of view, being drawn to another person who carries a different genetic profile makes sense for the next generation. We are more likely to be attracted on a biological level to those who have a different genetic makeup from what we ourselves have. And this makes sense for the strengthening of the human race. However, the biological attraction that is influenced by our hormonal and genetic profile does not give us the whole answer as to why we feel stronger chemistry with particular individuals.

From a biological point of view, we could say that because the male body contains testicles in which are cultivated millions of sperm on a daily basis, biologically this vehicle is naturally polygamous, seeking to "seed the world." This fact is evidence of a strong procreative force that has a drive of its own. This can also affect our experience attraction to others—for example, when the force is stronger, we feel more drawn to sex. From a purely biological level, if we were only mammals then our sexual instincts would constitute the main force of our experience of attraction. In the male vehicle, it would be present as a drive to seed as much of the world as possible, for the sake of the continuation of the species.

Left to a purely biological purpose of procreation, the male would be driven to sex daily—whereas the female, who is only able to procreate monthly, would be driven to sex on a monthly basis. We generally don't choose to be in a relationship with another on the basis of purely biological drives; rather, we choose to "couple with" others for reasons such as compatibility and ideology.

Research shows that females are most likely to "cheat" on their monogamous partners when ovulating. It is during ovulation that this sexual–biological drive draws them to the other simply because this is when conception can take place. It appears that these biological drives, as well as the chemistry we may feel with another human being, are not matters that we can dictate for ourselves. They arise from within the bodily system. We don't have a choice about them; we only have a choice as to whether or not we act upon them.

Sexual chemistry is not the only aspect of a human being that causes us to be attracted to another. We can also recognize the social conditioning that plays a role in what we perceive as attractive or not. We are additionally influenced by our family and religious views to be drawn to certain others with whom we feel we can share our lives. It is interesting to recognize that we may be sexually drawn to one individual but not want to share our life with that person. We would not want to include her or him in our family life; we are happy to have sex with that person but not want to bring her or him "home to meet mum." Here, the social aspect of attraction is already impinging upon the biological aspect of our attraction to another.

Individuals are also exposed to the influence of their families, as well as that of the popular culture and the community. The life body bears the blood bond, the hereditary stream. This body, or sheath, is our link to the community through the life we share with one another. Although we are socially engaged through our soul life, we live together and share the life sphere through our life body. All throughout our development, a strong force of conditioning exerts its influence upon our life body through all the people with whom we share our community of life.

Social conditioning also determines the gender roles that are assigned to the different bodily vehicles. These roles change according to the collective understanding of each community, and therefore various communities will express this differently according to their understanding thus far. The more a community works out of the forces of the "self-consciousness soul age," the less gender conditioning will be present. Even in communities where gender-stereotyped roles are assigned less frequently, it's often surprising to young people to realize just how great a role social conditioning plays in what they think are their free, individual impulses of attraction. But as they begin to explore the effects of social conditioning in their lives and those of others, the reality of this influence can often become clear to them. They begin to recognize that what they find to be sexually attractive has been stimulated by popular culture. They become aware of how the various trends of bodily shapes and sizes have had an influence on them.

It can be quite alarming for them to recognize how they have been influenced to feel drawn to individuals with certain looks. Social conditioning plays a significant role in attraction, from the superficial effect it has in predisposing us to feel attracted to people whose bodies are shaped in a certain way, to the deeper social conditions that work in our collective psyche.

When born into different cultures, we are affected by those cultures' ideas of attractiveness. In the midst of the way social conditioning affects us, if we are to become free in relation to our experiences of attraction, then we need to try and see what is drawing us to another human being. We are more likely to experience greater attraction to those who have positions in the culture that are deemed attractive. In the West, positions of power, positions of authority, wealth, and fame all add to the conditioned experience of what we find attractive in the other. This may be why, when a well-known personality stated, essentially, "When you're famous, you can do anything sexual toward others and get away with it," it was not outrageous to the majority of Americans, even though for many individuals within that society it was unbelievable to imagine that something like this could be culturally acceptable.

The culture is the outcome of our collective consciousness. Each community has its own collective consciousness, and this consciousness affects the inner life of each individual in that community. Further, each individual in the community has an effect on the collective consciousness for that community. The weight of the balance falls with the majority; in order to bring change to the practical life, the majority of the collective must be ready for change.

It is often shocking for some individuals when they see certain errors occurring that appear to be acceptable to the collective whole. The collective consciousness does not develop through the "political correctness" of what we want the other to think we believe; rather, the collective consciousness actually reveals to us the deeper beliefs of the community—even though these naturally do not equate to the deeper beliefs of every individual within that community. We are all subjected to the collective consciousness, we are influenced by it, and we each impress upon it what genuinely lives within us.

However, what we impress upon the collective consciousness is not who we are in the sense of how we like to see ourselves, but rather, how we truly are in our unconscious and subconscious thinking and feeling. If we merely suppress outwardly what actually lives in us as our thoughts and feelings, it does not change the collective atmosphere, because this atmosphere will reveal what lies hidden in the human being.

We see this particularly around "political correctness." We may wear a face on our personality that expresses a belief in equality for all, but how we truly feel—what lives in the depths of our souls—is what actually impresses itself upon the collective consciousness. This affects the abiding community life. And this is why so many individuals feel that extreme racism and sexism are still present in the world, even though outwardly we may have the impression that it has changed. Those who experience the error can recognize that the impression of change is, in part, only a so-called political change. Political correctness and the implementing of the correct social programs will not change the depths of the human soul. The atmosphere of the collective consciousness will not truly change until the fundamental social attitude of the majority of the community has changed.

From the time adolescents each become members of the wider community and emerge from being held as children within the family life, they become responsible for what they add to the collective consciousness. It is at this stage that each individual adolescent begins to participate in and contribute to the collective atmosphere with the depths of his or her being.

Adolescents add to the collective consciousness, and this is why it is especially important to educate adolescents directly about the effects and consequences of gender conditioning and stereotyping. It is an important part of the social education that needs to be taken up in homes and schools. Research on these themes shows us that domestic violence is directly linked to gender inequality. But this inequality goes much deeper than what we can see as the outwardly manifest consequences of dominance on a physical or soul level.

Working with gender prejudices is harder than we tend to think, because they live below the threshold of our consciousness; they are impressed upon the other without us even needing to say anything. Many young people experience the errors living in their teachers. It is not always a matter of overt stereotyping, such as a male teacher saying to young female students who are gathered to talk together, "Are you girls gossiping about boys?" It can be the deeper beliefs about male and female roles that the teacher holds and lives. The problem is not the role or position in which individuals happen to have been placed, but rather the idea that they should be placed there on account of having particular sexual organs. Someone's home life might look like a 1950s stereotype, and yet this home life will still be working out of the forces of the "self-consciousness soul" if the individuals are making choices out of themselves rather than being burdened by genital-related limitations of what they are allowed to do with their lives. Young children may love the traditionally "girl"- or "boy"-defined toys that society assumes they will like as girls or boys, and yet still be expressing their individual wants and wishes. The essential thing is not how it looks on the outside, but what is taking place in terms of mutual respect and consideration for the individual—both as they are now and in light of the continuously developing individuality growing within them.

Being defined by our gender or sexuality is not only a repressive force that comes from outside us. It also involves an inner aspect—namely, materialistic thinking, which provokes me to conflate my sexuality with my individuality. Some schools even set up programs dividing the children by their sexual characteristics and asking them questions like, "What do girls want to know about boys?" They think they are being "modern," but the adolescents can experience, even if not fully consciously, that they are being defined by their sex instead of their individuality. It is very important that we keep students together if we wish to address the unhealthy gender stereotypes that continually affect them. We should avoid such games and questions that reinforce gender conditioning; instead, we should attempt to bring their awareness to the error of questions like this—questions presuming that all boys would have the same questions about girls, and vice versa. Such questions expose the educators' limitations and undermine the individual students by reinforcing the collectivist opinion as to what is "normal and not normal." This does not elicit the individuality but rather has the potential to suppress it.

Young people are far more aware of this than we tend to think, but we will be unable to guide and educate them unless we are able to consciously hold the higher picture that they carry within themselves. With this higher picture, they themselves express, "It's not my concern who you get into bed with or what your desires are in this area; but what I want to know is who you are, what you think about, and what interests you." This is the gesture that we all need to be holding today, as what lives in us is unconsciously shared with those around us through the collective consciousness.

The sharing with others around us of what lives in our deeper inner being also takes place in the context of all one-on-one relationships. A teacher who holds a strong awareness of a child's spiritual growth has an effect on the child that is different from that of a teacher who would just like to get home and is in the teaching profession only for a job.

The people we spend our time with have a strong impact on which beliefs develop within us. This is especially the case in childhood when we cannot correct the errors in the environment around us; we just have to bear them, and in some cases, suffer them. This of course leads to great suffering for those who carry impulses within themselves that do not reflect the conditioning of the wider community.

Our individualized inner life also plays a big role in terms of what attracts us to others. Our inner life of attraction is often more emotionally based and located in our feeling life. It is here that young people can easily have "crushes" on others; it is here that we have the experience of "falling in love." The experience of being inwardly consumed in our feeling life by attraction to another human being can be overwhelming for young people. Our emotional attraction to another can also feel as if it is out of our hands, just as our biological attraction often is.

Falling in love or having a crush on another human being can also become an even greater experience of disturbance that goes against the social conditioning of what is deemed acceptable by the surrounding community. It can go against what you "should" or "shouldn't" experience and who you "can" or "cannot" have a crush on.

> Out beyond ideas of wrong-doing and right-doing,
> there is a field. I'll meet you there. (Rumi)[14]

We can even have crushes on people with whom we would not want a relationship. For instance, a student might have a crush on the teacher. We can have crushes on people with various sexual orientations. We can have crushes on others whose bodies are either similar or very different from our own. Having a crush on another individual or falling in love is not necessarily enough to distinguish our own sexual orientation.

This aspect of our attraction can be very powerful in determining what is taking place within our inner world. Are we drawn to the other's individual capacities, drawn to something that lives in them that may be missing in ourselves? Or are we drawn to how we feel in ourselves around them? And if so, what in us is being soothed, comforted, or eased when around them? Or am I being drawn to familiar inner experiences and patterns? With this type of attraction, we sometimes have no idea what draws us. And when it coincides with physical as well as social elements of attraction to the other, then such situations can be even less clear. However, we know that this elusive element of attraction is there in and of itself, because we can also be attracted to individuals with whom we do not want a sexual connection, or with individuals who do not fit socially acceptable conditions.

The other aspect of attraction, which we become increasingly aware of as we evolve our own being, is that we are attracted to others that support our development and our evolving. It is not so much that we necessarily have a lot in common with another individual, but it is recognized that in the relationship with that other, we can become more and they can become more because of the relationship. We can recognize that there is growth and development for both individuals just in the fact of knowing each other. It can be very disturbing when we fall in love with someone who is not good for our development—when we are emotionally connected to someone who diminishes our confidence or our growth and thriving.

Young people recognize that there can be no regrets about a relationship that "breaks down" if there has been growth and development through being together. The gratitude for who the other is in one's life continues even when there is pain in the act of letting go. Beyond the external relationship, the benefits of the time together live on inwardly. It's extraordinary to see how young people today have such a strong awareness of relationships that evolve and support growth and development, versus relationships that bring about diminishing and limiting experiences. They will often express that this other person "gets them." This experience is very significant to their ability to find connection in the world out of a strong sense of self.

When discussing these levels of attraction with young people, we can deepen the discussion between the ages of fourteen and sixteen. By age sixteen, all have begun to have some experiences of this nature within themselves. One of the main reasons to educate them together in a group of various ages is so that we can have greater social understanding for the other individuals in our lives and in the community. If we're able to perceive what takes place in ourselves, we can also begin to perceive and understand what may be taking place in others, even if it is quite different from our own experience.

As is true of other areas of attraction, we often seek those with forces and capacities that we do not possess ourselves. At the same time, the deeper aspect of such an attraction shows us that we are attracted to those with whom we can deeply converse. In these conversations, in both listening and speaking, we can gain greater clarity within ourselves about our relation to the world around us.

This aspect of attraction is incredibly significant in our age: to find others with whom, through conversation, we can extend ourselves in a creative way toward a greater understanding of the world around us. When two individuals are able to "sync together," and when the thinking that takes place between them is more than the thinking that would take place for each one alone, then they find a life teacher in their friend.

This requires an intimacy of our consciousness with the consciousness of the other. We begin to share concepts and what they mean to us in a deep way with each other. The thoughts that arise from such conversations take us into the future of our development. We can feel uplifted by the conversation, feeling that it raises us into our own greater possibilities of being. And at the same time, we can feel that, through bringing ourselves to the other, our own individuality is expressed and clarified, making it more understandable to ourselves.

We have all undoubtedly experienced times when aspects of our being are being pulled and attracted in ways that other aspects of our being do not wish to go, leaving us feeling torn. We also surely know of relationships that function in ways dramatically different from what we ourselves have experienced in our relationships. Some relationships work well without any sexual intimacy; other relationships "sing" based on sexual intimacy, but there is very little friendship. There are long-term relationships where each recognizes, as difficult as the relationship may be, that it is the right path for the growth and development of both individuals—and on the other hand, we have long-term relationships that endure for purely social or economic reasons. The configurations of what takes place in relationships are incredibly varied.

There are some relationships, however, in which one feels that the other "ticks all the boxes." One feels that one is sexually attracted to the other, that one want to live a life and build a life with that individual, that one has fallen in love with that individual, and that this individual is a part of one's evolving and developing independent life path. Such a relationship is often an ideal, which allows us to recognize that the fullness of life can be supported and expressed through it. However, each of these relationships is unique to those individuals within it. We, as the community, can best support others in achieving this ideal through not assessing the attractions we see around us in terms of what we think is right or wrong.

All young people experience some form of conflict among the various levels of attraction. The experience of conflict is a way of developing self-awareness and also of coming to understand the potential of a relationship. One of the greatest among the difficulties and challenges they may face is when they fall in love with someone who is not good for their development.

It is a common experience for young people to find conflict within themselves due to the various levels of attraction, but falling in love with someone and discovering that being with that person lessens our confidence, or diminishes who we are and prevents our independence and growth, is extremely hard. This is even more difficult when the person we are attracted to is not socially accepted by the group or community that we're living with. The hardest experience of all is when what lives inwardly as these various aspects of attraction and love are in conflict with our own selves.

Through the unfolding and the interplay of these various levels of attraction, we may also begin to understand more deeply the nature of our individual experiences of attraction to others; and our sexual orientation will not always be what we ourselves want it to be.

The complexity of attraction is different in each individual; but by understanding the various levels of attraction, we can also understand how we're developing as human beings. Another one of the great unifying aspects of all spiritual paths is the recognition of the significance of love in our human development and our development toward the spiritual world. Attraction may be the first glimpse of the potential for love.

Each of the four levels of attraction—biological drives, social commonality, emotional connection, and shared consciousness—often begin with interest or desire, but can also develop into qualities of genuine selfless love. Even though each of these four forms of attraction can of course be exclusive of love, they are likewise potentially cultivators of love.

Wild Forces

> There are beautiful wild forces within us.
> Let them turn the mills inside
> and fill sacks
> that feed even
> heaven.
>
> (St. Francis of Assisi)[15]

These four levels of attraction can become four aspects of love if we ourselves cultivate them through the practice of bringing love to them. First, we have sexual attraction, which is expressed in our sexual chemistry and biological drives. It can be expressed in sensual love toward another when we stay present and connected to the physical intimacy we are sharing. We also have social attraction, which is really expressed by what is given as a picture of attractiveness by our larger culture, family, or peer group. This quality of attraction can develop more strongly over time through living in partnership or raising children with the intention of supporting care and harmony for all in the "family"; this is then expressed as a blood-bond form of love.

Then, in our inner life, we have feeling-based attraction; this is the emotional quality of our attraction to the other, and it can come to expression in the form of having deep interest, having a crush, or falling in love. This soul love is growing in us as a collective humanity, and many people experience that such experiences blossom into deep friendship–love.

As an independent, individual "I"-being, experiences of attraction to others are also experiences of attraction to the development and evolution of our consciousness of the other. This love, known as *universal love,* is still at its beginning stages.[16]

When allowed to unfold naturally, these four levels of attraction can lead each of us to grow more mature in the capacity for love. It is a part of our spiritual task to discover how our individuality lives in relationship to the spiritual capacities of love. Through our own thinking, feeling, and will impulses, we can perceive the extent to which we are developing our capacity to love. It is also a part of our task to support this quest in others around us.

It may be difficult for some to recognize that, although the experiences of others are often different from our own, these experiences may still be genuine and true. However, at the very least, we must be able to see such experiences as an expression of other people's processes of working toward the realization of their individuality.

In All Things

It was easy to love God in all that
was beautiful.

The lessons of deeper knowledge, though,
instructed me
to embrace God in all things.
(St. Francis of Assisi)[17]

If we're to be a part of the evolving impulses, we need to continue to work toward supporting freedom and cultivating love for the other as well as for ourselves. Developing freedom is the most important task of this age. Without freedom, no genuine spiritual love will be able to come into life though the human being. We may not agree with ways others live life but, purely out of love and respect for the independence of the other's free will, we must agree that they should be free to find their own way. Further, for all we know, they may be more connected to the progressive spiritual impulses than we think.

No One Knows His Name

No one
knows his name—
a man who lives on the streets
and walks around in
rags.

Once I saw that man in a dream.
He and God were constructing
an extraordinary
temple.
(St. Francis of Assisi)[18]

No great changes in the capacities of love and freedom can come about on earth unless the majority of individuals in the community can change their relationships to love and freedom. Supporting individual freedom and the development of love among all other members of the community—supporting their individual liberation—serves to support the liberation of the whole community.

3

CREATING CHANGE THROUGH
THE FEMININE AND MASCULINE

Gender-based sex education—sex education that focuses primarily on biology, the mechanics of sex, and sexually transmitted diseases—fails to convey how the less conscious attitudes of sexual discrimination and gender conditioning bring about a socially transmitted "dis-ease" with far-reaching consequences to the wellbeing of adolescents. This affects not only their sexual health, but also the health of their soul life, and these effects often continue into adulthood.

Healthy education lays the ground for young people to grow into adults who will stay connected to the inner realities and deeper dimensions of life in the living soul world. If we ourselves have not received this grounding, then we will have need of reeducation of the soul.

There are three main ways to support the individual's process of learning to experience the living soul world, and these are effective both in preparing young people for harmonious adult consciousness and in reeducating the life of our own soul as adults. The first of these is through the capacity of becoming more sensitive to the impressions of the sense world. Becoming aware of the various effects sensory impressions have on our inner life serves to develop our soul's sensitivity into an organ of perception for realities hidden from the everyday perception of the material world.

The foundations of this capacity are best supported and cultivated in the developing child through an education that is able to sculpt the soul space by means of a rich process of learning centered in meaningful experiential education, authentic inner understanding, and artistic perceiving. Sculpting the soul space in the developing children requires us to help them to maintain their sensitivity in relation to the natural world, and to protect this sensitivity from becoming blunted through intensive screen watching or cramming them full of facts that need to be regurgitated. Depending on the age of a child, we may offer various ways of growing his or her inner world—from telling fairy tales to younger ones, to supporting the individualized interest in the world of older children. In all ages, we are attempting to present the world to the *inner life* of the child, rather than to the brain-oriented thinking alone as if we were programming a computer.

The second way that we can serve to sculpt the soul space of our students or to reeducate our own souls as adults is by using our own inner world of soul activity to explore the nature of what arises from the intentions we cultivate. In the case of the adult, this requires a powerful cultivation of inner forces that are strengthened not by following the impressions made on the sense organs, but by developing an independent "soul-scape" that can be activated at will within our inner world through our concentrated soul forces. We can thereby create sense-free images and experiences out of our own inner activity.

The ground for this activity is laid in growing children by applying a concentrated effort toward learning various activities that contain their own expressions of lawfulness—for example, playing a musical instrument, scientific thinking, or mathematical problem solving. Each of these activities requires children to deepen their power of understanding inwardly and to discover how they can develop new inner capacities by applying the necessary concentrated effort.

The third and most intensive way that we, as adults, can sculpt or reeducate the soul is by cultivating a deeper relationship with one's own inner life—cultivating the capacity to enter an "inner space" where deep contemplation or meditation can take place between the inner world and the subject of our enquiry. This involves working to allow new thoughts and inspirations to awake within us. Efforts applied toward this end lead us to become capable of allowing the direct revelations from the higher worlds to impress themselves upon our own soul, revealing to us the mysteries of these worlds.

The potential for this capacity is seeded in childhood through helping the children to cultivate reverence and awe toward the world around them. It is important not to intellectualize what they see through over-analyzing it or giving information too early, but rather to allow play and wonder to be their main educators. We can support this development in the children through providing them inner space to dream and imagine, as well as allowing the child space to "just be." It can also be supported in the older child through allowing deeper exploration of the world and its wonders, in the sense of seeing the evolution of the human being both from the perspective of inspiring individual biographies as well as transformative world history—seeing the evolving and progressive development of individuals and societies.

As adults, if this ground within us has been hindered by the anaesthetizing world, we can regain it through reeducating our souls. If it has not been altogether lost in childhood, then our further soul education will be made much easier. Even still, most of us already have inner hindrances, as we all contend with aspects in ourselves that need evolving. Soul reeducation is needed in order to combat the hindrances. We can bring this to ourselves through the process of inner training. However, new soul education streaming directly from the spiritual world requires that we overcome the inner hindrances in order not to block this connection.

> Human beings today confront the greatest test of strength: the test of their ability to work in freedom toward the spirit, which approaches them of its own accord if they do not shut themselves off from it. The spiritual can no longer reveal itself to human beings in all kinds of subconscious and unconscious processes. The time has come for human beings to receive the light of the spirit through a free inner deed. (Rudolf Steiner, "How to Listen to the Spirit")[19]

In order for us to be able to receive the impressions given from the higher realms in a way that is unimpeded by our own subjective coloring, we must be able to sacrifice the content of our personal soul life and allow ourselves to be permeated purely by the living soul world of cosmic thinking, feeling, and will impulses.

Only a being living entirely in materiality could think that it loses itself through sacrifice; no—an elevating, enriching development is linked to sacrifice in service of universal evolution. (Rudolf Steiner, *The Astral World*)[20]

Each individual adds to the collective consciousness that steers the whole of humanity forward. Supporting the evolving of individuals supports in turn the evolution of the whole. The ability for individuals to grow and learn abundantly through life, and abundantly to share their inner capacities and talents with the world, requires a healthy inner balance among the various aspects of our own being. We all want to live a vibrant, inwardly fulfilling lives that can also be expressed outwardly in the form of an individually created life.

Somewhere inside us, we know that the human being is not destined for the gray, lifeless existence that a purely material engagement with the world tends to offer. We are not to become slaves of materialism; we are actually destined for the fullness of life on all levels of being. It is through glimpses into our continued connection to the spiritual world that we can most readily perceive this possibility.

Because materialistic thinking is dominant in the world, our relationship to this ever-present spiritual connection is blunted while we are immersed in physical reality—even though our pledge to come into incarnation was made from a more living experience of connectedness. All incarnated beings had at one point decided that they wanted to be counted as members of those who act as a bridge between the uncreated spiritual existence and the created world of sense perception. Each wants to reenliven and evolve the created world through the forces of spiritual life. But inevitably, in the anaesthetizing world as it exists today, we forget who we are and why we're here, and we are impressed upon by the idea that our life is primarily about our personal selves.

> It is precisely from the moment in history when the waves of materialism are rising higher than ever, that the strongest force from the spiritual world to have ever willed to enter human life is seeking to enter it. (Rudolf Steiner, "How to Listen to the Spirit")[21]

Deep below our personal experience of who we think we are, we remain connected to the greater forces of eternal spiritual activity. But for many individuals, the experience of spiritual reality soon becomes suspended and displaced in the wake of physical realities—the greater spiritual life quiets and becomes dormant until it comes to rest below the threshold of the individual's consciousness.

This circumstance is brought about in no small part because of the changes in the collective atmosphere, and because of the way we treat the growing child. The majority of individuals experience an upbringing that supports the development of only certain capacities in their being, or that supports the development of their capacities in an imbalanced way. This generally happens not because we want to cause disturbances, but because we ourselves are not fully awake to the new flow of consciousness now calling upon us to awaken what is individual in each child. It is often through the influences of tradition and culture that we tend to rest on past forms of educating the new generation; but mainly, this unawareness of the needs of the future is due to our own conditioning.

Inevitably, this situation leads children to conform aspects of their own inner world to the imbalanced realities that surround them externally. These outer, external hindrances passed on through the unconsciousness of others must then become our thoughts, feelings, and beliefs. All internalized untruths grow into internal hindrances that we later have to correct as adults. Even though these errors may have been passed on to the next generation, as the poet Rainer Maria Rilke says, "like a sealed letter, without even knowing it,"[22] they are nevertheless now our own inner hindrances. And we will propagate similar hindrances onto the generations to come unless we are prepared to awaken to the new impulses that bring in the pictures of evolution willed by the spiritual world. Within our inner world of soul, we are not as "closed off" and separated from the world around us as we are when experiencing life primarily through the sheath of our physical body.

The soul world unites with the collective consciousness and is educated by it. The soul world is also capable of uniting with the spiritual worlds. The inner soul world is the bridge through which we are linked to the cosmic forces of the spiritual world. In both directions, our thinking, feeling, and will are not entirely our own. In our thinking, we are not bound entirely to our separate thoughts. We can see and recognize that we are open to the collective consciousness, and that we are not entirely sealed off from it. If human beings were to think new thoughts that would serve to support the evolution of humanity, then they must connect with the cosmic thinking that can imbue them with the thoughts of spiritual consciousness. When we're connected with these spiritual realities in our thinking, we do not say, "I think this or that," but rather it would be closer to the truth to say "It thinks." We are thinking with the world thoughts.

Very many individuals have the experience that, in their contemplative thinking life, something else thinks with them. They recognize that they have thoughts that are beyond their personal capacity. They recognize that the quality of the thought has an objective nature, and that this objective nature has now entered into their own common thinking. It is one of the most extraordinary experiences of spiritual connection to awake each morning and think in the direction of our deeper questions, and to experience thoughts thinking within our own thinking that are so much fuller and more alive than the merely reflective thoughts prompted by the grey material world could ever be.

What lives in the human being's feeling is connected to the world soul. When we experience the outer world, we take in the world around us and allow the world to inform us about its nature. If I did not have a capacity for feeling–experiencing, then I would be incapable of growing and learning. Our feeling–experiencing is not isolated and separated as is the case with the physical body, but it is in constant relationship to the world soul. Here, the outer appearances of the things of the world not only reveal themselves to our senses, but they also move us, giving something to us—and we experience on a feeling level what is in front of us.

Behind the sense perceptible object that we look at, we can experience how our activity of perceiving it affects our inner world, bringing about certain movements and changes. From this inner awareness experience, we learn more about the object than we would through the basic experience of sense perception alone. The world soul reveals itself both within us and outside of us. What lives and weaves behind the sensory impression that is taken into the brain also has a more subtle effect on the soul, such that it evokes in us a simultaneous experiencing–feeling of the sense impression. We could say that the activity behind the object of our perception communes with the soul activity within our own being. This activity informs us of more than what the senses or brain alone can inform us of.

This deepened capacity to be aware of the activity both within and outside of myself is something that needs to be developed in all individuals as a continuation of our evolving. Two individuals could be watching the sunrise, and one may experience deep effects and be moved by the beauty, while the other may not be affected at all. Two people can cross the ocean in a boat, living night after night under the majesty of the night sky; one of them may be entirely changed by the experience, whereas the other may show little or no inner movement through having taken such a journey.

Our capacity to let the world in and allow it to affect us depends on whether this aspect of our soul being has been supported and cultivated, or suppressed and denied. Much depends on whether we have been supported in a way that enables us to be deeply moved by the world around us, and to allow ourselves to express the movement of feeling arising from the experiences—or whether we have been blunted through focusing too heavily on the strictly material aspect of our perceptions or told that any perceptions other than the material expresses a wrong way of being. Or, we may have been told that we should not feel in this way, that we should not be so sensitive—and so we divert or block our inner experiences. The world soul feels and it is this feeling in us that allows us to be deeply affected by the world. The esoteric expression "She feels" gives rise to this ability to be permeated by the world in a way reaching beyond what we know already within our individual soul, and to be affected by what penetrates us in such a way that we may learn and grow through this encounter with the wisdom of the world soul.

What lives in the human being's will is intimately connected to the world spirit. The will has the capacity for creative activity, for bringing something that lives within me out into the world and making it manifest in the external world around me. A macrocosmic version of this will activity also takes place through the world spirit, the creator. If we are able to change the world, as we are all able to do through bringing changes individually, then we must actively bring what we think and feel into the world around us. We must summon the creative will that we know to be living within us, in order to implement what we believe needs to be given to the outer world.

Again, it is not merely we alone, with our separated forces of will, who are about to bring the good into the world around us, but it is also the force that is connected to the creative impulse of the spiritual world. The fact that individuals can enact what is good into the world is due to the fact that they have this connection to the creative spiritual being of "the will of the world," which is by nature good.

In and through us, the spiritual world can be thought and revealed, and then we may freely will it into the external world. We are always effecting change in the world from what lives in our thinking, feeling, and will impulses—but when we unite with the spiritual world, we are thereby changing the external world through the impulses given by the spirit. Esoterically, this is expressed as "He wills."

We all have both true and false thoughts, both beautiful and ugly feelings, and both moral and immoral impulses of will. In order to experience these thoughts, feelings, and will impulses, we must live with a connection to our deeper soul capacities, perceptions, and experiences. To transform what lives in us so that we can align our inner thoughts, feelings, and deeds to the truth, beauty, and goodness of the spiritual world, we need to choose this path of inner work ever more consciously as our independent, individual freedom develops.

> Nothing but the will to lead life in a spiritual way, the will to allow spiritual decisions, spiritual motivations, to play a part in what we do in the physical world, can make humanity truly healthy again. (Rudolf Steiner, "How to Listen to the Spirit")[23]

We can readily recognize the true, the harmonious, and the moral in the world. However, we still choose independently how to make use of our lives and what to do with the forces we have. We may choose to use them toward gaining an ever more conscious relationship to the spiritual world.

We each already have living within us some principles of truth and spiritual life, in the form of our ideals. The ideals we bring with us into the world may be called "spiritual principles" or "universal laws," and they are a part of our own eternal being.

They are called "universal" as these laws govern not only human beings, but also other forms of spiritual consciousness. In most spiritual schools, we are instructed about these laws in some way—or about what in earthly terms we might call "doing the good" or "morality."

Even if we're not conscious of harboring traces of these ideals within us, we all fundamentally have access to the various universal laws. They come to expression in the physical world around us, and in this way they reflect back to us the underlying world of spiritual life. They go by different names among the various world religions and spiritual practices, but they are familiar to most human beings in the form of healthy human characteristics.

Although it is difficult to clothe these laws in simple phrases, one of the most commonly known laws could be stated as, "To support the progression of another being is a good thing."

This law is lived by the progressive forms of spiritual consciousness that support humanity, as well as by human beings who know this law in the heart of their being. We see this law expressed in numerous faiths: in Buddhism, Christianity, Islam, and in the various esoteric schools—as well as in the New Age movement.

One of the most difficult things to reconcile in our humanness is the fact that it is possible for us to fall short of the universal laws living in our deeper hearts and minds, because we are able to follow other threads in our nature—threads such as greed.

Those who live with a focused spiritual striving may suffer when their own ideals are not realized. We do not need a church or doctrine to tell us what lives in our hearts and minds; we already recognize the moral truth of our ideals ourselves. Our church and our beliefs, or our spiritual striving, only confirm to us what already lives in our hearts and minds. They are already instilled in us because they are one with the spirit in us. Through them, we come to recognize the spirit in us.

These universal laws are our individual compass for living a truthful, harmonious, and morally sound life. Along with the various universal laws, in most spiritual schools there is also a recognition that at some point we will eventually return to some form of a spiritual existence. Until we do, we can make conscious progress in our relationship with the divine spiritual world through certain forms of spiritual practice, worship, prayer, and so forth. This means that, even in earthly life, we can utilize our individual "I"-force in order to grow into a deeper relationship with the spiritual world, and therefore to directly attain and live more fully within the principles of life in the spiritual world.

As we inwardly grow into deeper spiritual realities, we learn more fully of the universal laws; and as we participate in spiritual life, we grow in our capacity to live these universal laws during our outer earthly existence.

Human beings, because they each have an individualized will, live these laws in way that are unique to their own individuality. In and through each one of us, these laws come to expression uniquely in the world. All spiritual laws are lived by all the progressive spiritual consciousnesses, but only slowly, over time, does the human being learn to live these laws out of themselves, in freedom and independence. If we were unfree beings, we would be bound by religious codes to follow the laws given to us; however, in time, as we become increasingly awake to our individuality, we can no longer follow what is good blindly, but must choose it with active will.

As we progress further into the self-consciousness soul age, we will begin to see where we really are as a collective humanity. Even if we have a strong faith or religious life, we are no longer subject to the authority of following what is given subconsciously and unconsciously by the spirit—we are now free to live these laws independently of any external or internal authority.

Some of these laws are not as well understood by our human consciousness at present; for some of these laws, we have yet to grow into them or "choose" them. One of those universal laws could be expressed as, "The more you have the more you give." This is a law that is lived by all spiritual beings that work for the progression of humanity—but it is not yet a moral law that the individuals working for most corporations choose to include in their mission statement. In the programs implemented for the distribution of wealth, we are seeing a demise of the working of this principle, which was once upheld as a matter of course through the subconscious or intuitive knowing of the past. As our individual and independent self-conscious grows, so does the possibility of serving only ourselves. Only when human beings recognize the truth of spiritual realities *in freedom* can we abide by them in earthly life.

Along with these universal laws, which are growing within us, there are also developmental stages that humanity as a whole must grow into. We do not come to live the heavens on earth immediately. In our developing freedom, we can also choose not to live the heavens on earth. However, through the course of our evolution, through our evolving and deepening capacities, we can learn to bring the spiritual realities into earthly existence.

Because we do this in freedom and out of our individuality, we will always do this in ways that are individual and unique to us. The individuality always makes its mark upon various aspects of what we are able to bring into the world. If we have not individualized it, it is not yet ours. We can see how the individuality makes its mark on the physical body, right down to our individual fingerprints—we see an expression of our uniqueness, our individual quality "marking" this is as our body. This individual expression unfolds in the realm of the life body through the collection of memories of our life that we maintain. Two individuals can find themselves in the exact same circumstances or event, but they may remember the events in a unique way. Our memory of our lives and the events we experienced are an expression of our individual nature within the life body. We find the mark of the individuality in our inner soul life in the experience of conscience. We all know what conscience is, but we experience it individually—and we each have a different quantity and quality in terms of how conscience works into our lives. In the context of our soul life, our individuality is imprinted and comes to expression by our conscience's ability to alert us to our potential or actual misdeed.

In our independent, individual consciousness, our individuality comes to expression in how we utilize the transformative capacity that lives within each of us. We're equal in terms of the capacities available to us, but we are unique in how we choose to cultivate, order, and express those capacities through our individual utilizing of them.

Our peripheral personality places us into the egotism of our self, often acting like a guard: defending ourselves against the penetration of anything different from ourselves, or feeling hypersensitive to the opinions of others. Most adolescents move through some form of experience of this within themselves and in their peers. The personality creates separation between the other and myself, allowing for the experiences of both "selfness" and selfishness to arise. Something of the separation that occurs through this selfishness is useful, because it allows us to awaken to the reality of the individuality in a certain way, through the inner feeling of knowing *"I am an independent, individual, separate being."* But in our time, if we really want to bring the living realities of spiritual life back into the world out of the forces of freedom, then we as adults have to change our orientation from life being about ourselves, to actually forgetting ourselves.

The spiritual realities of life awaken in our activity of forgetting our personal self. When we forget our personal self, but still remain aware out of the forces of the "I," then we can let our personality fall into the background and allow the spiritual world to enter in. This may be experienced in moments of spiritual activity during deep meditation, or when we rest in that tiniest, humble space and experience the vastness of consciousness; it can also happen when we feel the surrounding world of beings wanting to impress upon us. It can even come to us in our experiences in the world, whereby we allow ourselves to let "even mute things speak to us," informing us of who they are. Forgetting ourselves is necessary in order to experience the spirit in the world. It is a necessity in order that we may enter higher spiritual worlds. To enter the spiritual realms that directly bestow revelation onto the human soul, we have to be able to forget ourselves. Forgetting ourselves, in whichever world we are working in, allows that world to enter us—it allows that world to impress upon us, to speak to us, to resound in us.

> We must be prepared at every moment that every object and every being can bring to us some new revelation. (Rudolf Steiner, *Knowledge of the Higher Worlds and Its Attainment*)[24]

The elements and ethers that create the substance and form of the externalized, created world around us are, like us, borne from the spirit. And when we forget ourselves and live into the deeper part of our own eternal being, then the spirit in all things becomes alive to us in its eternal spiritual aspect.

If we are judging the other, we are working out of our past and not out of the eternal part in us. It is essential that we don't judge this moment by a past experience, but rather allow the past to help us to see the new that lives in this moment. In forgetting, I begin to see the new. I begin to see what is coming into being now; I begin to see the creating of the Creator.

And so we move forward in the great Mystery, from forgetting to being able to recognize the creating—the creating that happens because new things are arising. In the seeing of the new, we are remembering the creative spirit. In this remembering, we are maintaining a continuous connection with the spiritual world. Through this connection with the wisdom and harmony of the living spiritual world, we can act out of it—and acting out of the spirit is the force of creation that we bring into the world.

The human being creates. The forces of creating that we are able to work with reflect what is available to us in the present moment. What we recognize as being available to our perception, or to our experience, represents the extent of our ability to connect with the wisdom and harmony of the living spiritual world.

That means that for each one of us, whatever is revealed to us directly from the spiritual world is the thing that we can bring to the earthly world—which, in itself, represents the uniting of our being with the Creator. To be able to bring something to the world through my own direct experience of the spirit is a matter of human creating. This creating is expressed through me in the thoughts that I convey, in word, and in my deeds within the world.

It's an extraordinary thing for human individuals to be able to communicate to other human beings, to communicate something of their living reality of spiritual life. In such communications, even if it is not said in spoken words, we plant spiritual seeds, healing seeds into the world.

We don't only communicate through the spoken world; but when we do communicate in this way, we have to consider what comes behind those words. The word is clearly the sound being formed, but what resounds behind the word actually changes the meaning of the words we speak entirely.

Even if I speak spiritual truths—if they are merely coming from my chattering personality, then they have no spiritual life to them. So even spiritual truths, such as "we are spiritual beings," can be empty unless the speaker has some genuine soul experience of what is indicated with these words.

> It makes a difference, surely, whether some popular orator says that humankind must "learn new lessons," or whether this is said by someone who knows that humanity's habits of artificial and shallow thinking have created such depths of false thoughts that these reach down into the very structure of the human nervous system. (Rudolf Steiner, "From Empty Phrase to Living Word")[25]

When the person who has genuine soul experiences says, "Humankind must learn new lessons," then what's contained in those words is totally different from the case of someone chattering those words from the periphery of themselves. What is contained in our words becomes our creative contribution to the enlivening of the spirit of the world. It makes a huge difference when what is contained in our words comes as a fruit of what has been lived through, activated, or revealed and impressed on us directly.

The spiritual revelations that are spoken from this source are then no longer a matter of the human being speaking alone. Every human being could say the same words without need of those revelations, but when we speak out of inner connection, we speak out of something greater than ourselves. The sounds of speech contain elements of the formative, living Word.

> We must fill our souls with what can really inspire us when we speak. We must find a way to make the heart speak through the lips. We must find a way to penetrate the words with our entire being. (Rudolf Steiner, "From Empty Phrase to Living Word")[26]

We must allow the world to speak to us, within our soul, so that we can be changed by it—but through our relationship with what is revealed to us in this way, we also speak *to* the world, and what we speak in turn changes the world. All evolution takes place through relationship. What we bring out of our inner soul makes a huge difference for the world, even for the "dumb" or "mute things." We can look out into this world with all of its "mute things," but if we are able to allow it to speak to us, then it becomes more alive. And if we speak to it with living soul, we also bring life to it.

> Every external revolution today, no matter how agreeable to whichever party or class, will lead us only into

the worst of blind alleys and inflict the most terrible misery on humanity, unless it is illumined by an inner revolution of the soul. This involves abandoning one's absorption in purely materialistic views and actively preparing to receive the spiritual wave that wants to pour down into human evolution as a new revelation. (Rudolf Steiner, "How to Listen to the Spirit")[27]

What we truly "say" to the world is what we actually have resounding within us—not the words that leave our lips with politically correct statements.

Some schools in the world are banning references to the students as "boys and girls," stating that we now have to call them "students" in order not to impress gender bias upon them. We may find it useful to change the words—we might need to change our language. And yet, it makes no difference to the freedom of the child whether we use the word "students" or the words "boys and girls" if the teacher still carries biases inwardly. It only makes a difference to the freedom of the child if the teacher inwardly knows that this external bodily representation cannot be thought of as the totality of the individual being in front of me. The bodily vehicle might express something of people's individuality in one of its aspects for one reason or another; but who they are and what they're here to do—how they need to express themselves—may be an entirely different matter. What an individual is here to bring may be different from what the community's collective consciousness thinks this "type of vehicle" should do, feel, or think.

We can go around with these so-called social laws, the new language of working with each other socially—just changing the chatter. So now we're politically happy with the chatter, but where is the revelation? Where is the inner change that actually now leaves others free in their individuality?

> However many times that a parrot might say a number of
>   things, will that make that true for the bird?
> So it is with many utterances about spiritual matters from
>   people; they just may never occur except in make-
>   believe, which probably won't pay the rent.
> Harness speech; let it become a windmill that can grind a
>   harvest.
> There is a pristine energy in sounds that come from
>   certain depths that can help split the atom
> if you can control them perfectly, which would mean your
>   words cease to harm, and always uplift, or at least
>   comfort.
> With our world so ripe for help, this is what our
>   relationship is at times about—
> *me increasing your power*, so you can bake a special
>   wheat, that can feed the various longings a refined
>   heart can know. (Hafiz)[28]

It is so unfortunate that many impulses from the spiritual world that want to lead us forward become materialistic in us. We descend into chatter instead of asking deeper questions, such as: What does it mean that human beings in our time are entering into life without such strongly one-sided male/female qualities? What does it mean that we have this new orientation, wherein there are many individuals not fixed in the polarity of male/female? What does it mean that many more individuals, upon entering into the world, do not identify with older forms of male/female stereotypes? If we could ask these questions, and if we could understand them with the help of listening to the inner spiritual revelations, then we would know that what is being asked of us is that we look beyond the merely external being, and seek instead the individual—that we seek for what constitutes their true self.

We would then know that the spirit is trying to awaken in us the realization that we must stop externalizing—to wake us up to the reality of the living spiritual being that dwells within each individual. Instead, what we often do is merely change the chatter, and yet think that we are making real human progress. What is truly contained in our words is not the mere fact of outer correctness or incorrectness, but rather our deeper inner life and beliefs. This is why those who are sensitive to these matters know that there is still deep racism and sexism occurring, even behind the "new" chatter. The chatter does not change the collective consciousness, nor does it transform imbalances within the collective society. Only those revelations of the spiritual reality of equality have a healing effect. It doesn't matter what words are spoken. What matters is the deeper being of who speaks the words.

> Then these words contain something healing—healing seeds. In our time, we are being asked to give the seeds that can awaken spiritual love, the reality of the Logos, in the world around us." (Rudolf Steiner, "From Empty Phrase to Living Word")[29]

We are blocked from these realities through the inner hindrances that we bear. However, we are not merely left to our inner hindrances without the capacity to do something about them. We can adjust what lives in us. Just as the "six subsidiary exercises" (described in chapter 2) work upon external hindrances, serving to block the negative effects of the collective consciousness on our own inner world, so do meditative and contemplative exercises work upon our internal hindrances, lessening their effect on our clear experience of the spiritual world and its guidance.

Many meditative exercises serve to align us with the spiritual realities we have lost touch with through material life, as well as preparing us for a relationship with the living spiritual world and the experiences that we may receive through that relationship. In order to do this, the soul life needs to be reeducated in that direction, through which we may commune with spiritual life and become aware of the dimensions of our relationship with the living spiritual world. As we grow into this reality, life itself changes for us. We become aware of just how much is still being bestowed upon the human race. We begin to see that we are still evolving, despite the great veil of materialism. We see how the next generation is coming with a new consciousness that brings with it continued hope in the progress of humanity. We begin to grow into the awareness of how assisted we are in our striving, and how we can connect directly with those guiding forces through our deeper soul activity.

VERSE FROM RUDOLF STEINER

In my thinking, world thoughts live,
in my feeling, world powers weave,
in my will, will beings work,

I will perceive myself
 In world thoughts,
I will experience myself
 In world powers,
I will create myself
 In beings of will.[30]

The path of transformation is actually not so much a path of my personal transformation, as it is a path of world transformation—a path toward reenlivening the world. We can work to understand these qualities and activities in ourselves in a new way by engaging with prescribed meditative exercises.

Both forms of inner exercise are necessary for us in order to bring about the required dynamic change in this area of gender conditioning and imbalances of the inner forces: the six subsidiary exercises help us to overcome the outer obstacles that are continuously being laid down in us through the collective consciousness, while the meditation exercise given here helps us to overcome the inner obstacles and awaken the slumbering forces that lie within. However we can only safely meditate once we have become awake to our own independent individuality; for most people, that happens in the early twenties, but the six subsidiary exercises can easily be started from age sixteen onward, once individuals can experience self-willed, objective consciousness of their own thinking, feeling, and will impulses, and not be bound to them only subjectively.

The "main exercise" below has been given in various versions in the many esoteric schools. It relates directly to the "middle-pillar exercise" of the Greek Mysteries, and the "tree-of-life exercises" of the Egyptian rites. However, the words used to activate the exercise evolve as our understanding and stage of development as human beings evolve. Rudolf Steiner gave this exercise to many students of the esoteric path as an inner practice. Its value will continue to be effective until the end of this age, when its words will change again. It can be useful to consider the way this exercise came to expression in other schoolings before the transition into the self-consciousness soul age, as this overview shows how the progression of human consciousness is met by the inner training in different ways over the course of time.

The exercise for our time, as given through Rudolf Steiner:

> I am
> It thinks [cosmic thinking]
> She feels [world soul]
> He wills [world spirit][31]

The exercise given in the old Greek Mysteries:

> *Ego Eimi* (I am)
> *Gnosis* (knowledge)
> *Sophia* (wisdom)
> *Zoe* (life)

The exercise given in the ancient Egyptian rites:

> *Nudjer ao* (The great God self-proclaimed)
> *Neb Iri Khet* (Lord Creator)
> *Sia* (God of knowledge and wisdom)
> *Neb Ankh* (Lord of life)

As citizens of the self-consciousness soul age, we now work with the words of power appropriate to our time: *I am, It thinks, She feels, He wills.*

The following preparation of knowledge about this exercise is given so that we may experience the centers being worked with, in order to make our own evaluation before taking up the practice. This will also serve us in seeing how the exercise develops over time in terms of the various changes that will take place within us.

First, we focus on the "third eye": the point between the eyebrows, at the root of the nose but a little way back into the interior of the forebrain. Here we experience the quality of "I"-consciousness. To do this, we inwardly look toward the point of the third eye, and concentrate our attention there for a few minutes, free from all other content. We just focus our attention to this spot of the body and see what we can perceive.

What is the first thing that comes in and disturbs the quality of the "I"-consciousness experience? Usually it is our thought life, because the thought life exists close to the "I."

Now concentrate on the second point: the throat center, at the center of the neck or larynx. What is it that begins to stir as we do this?

What is it that comes in to disturb this quality? A quality of movement or activity from below this center starts to distract us. Now, if we try to concentrate on the heart's center—in the center of the chest, between the breasts—what is it that takes us away from being present?

The last center is located in the region of the navel. This is the will center of the body. In spiritual science, this will force is designated as a masculine force, as the "world spirit." The activity of bringing something through us in order to change and affect the world around us—this is our masculine activity. In meditative practice, it is esoterically identified as the activity, "He wills," which connects us to the world spirit, to the Creator spirit.

In the feeling life, we allow ourselves to be penetrated by the other—and this links us to the world soul, esoterically identified as "She feels" in the heart region.

The esoteric identifies cosmic thinking as "It thinks" in the throat center.

The individual expression of the eternal spirit is identified as the "I am," and is located at the third eye.

In this exercise, we will learn to focus our forces upon each center; then, we inwardly sound the words of power pertaining to each center. We can gradually develop discernment as to what these qualities are, and we can work to ensure that we ourselves are developing in all centers equally. We can learn to orient ourselves to whichever quality is required to meet in the best way any given situation. Regardless of our developmental stage, we need to continue to experience these qualities and develop them within us to make progress on the ever-unfolding path of inner development.

What follows are the practical instructions for working with this meditation. The meditative "main exercises" are preceded by cultivating the right soul state for entering into them in such a way that they may be fruitful and transformative. This begins with developing a restful state of soul, unattached to everyday thinking, feeling, and willing. Once we have achieved this state of restfulness of soul (see *The Inner Work Path* for these exercises),[32] we may utilize a verse and immerse ourselves in it with our thinking, feeling, and will so that nothing else but the verse exists in the content of our inner life for those few minutes. An example of a complimentary verse would be the thoughts given earlier in this chapter—however, we can work with any verse that serves to unfold a greater understanding of the life of the soul within the spiritual world, thus directing the soul toward purely spiritual content.

> *In my thinking, world thoughts live,*
> *in my feeling, world powers weave,*
> *in my will, will beings work,*
>
> *I will perceive myself*
>   *In world thoughts,*
> *I will experience myself*
>   *In world powers,*
> *I will create myself*
>   *In beings of will.*[33]

Then we may follow this by entering the main exercise. The best body position for this main exercise is to be comfortably seated on a chair, with the left hand in the lap, palm facing upward, and the right hand laying in the left also with palm facing upward.

We breathe in for a count of two, three, or four—whatever is comfortable. The length of the in-breath is up to us (our comfort level will increase in duration as we become familiar with the exercise). Then we breathe out for double the count of the in-breath. If we breathe in for a count of two, then we breathe out for a count of four. During this time, we do not focus on the various centers or focal points of the body, but we focus only on the activity of the in- and out-breathing. During the next period of time, after the breath is exhaled, we leave the breath outside the body for three times the length of the in-breath; while the breath is being held out, we focus on the point between the eyes while inwardly speaking (or sounding, reverberating) the words "I am." It is these words, directed to this focal point, that serve to organize and awaken this particular center of the body. In this center, the transformative power of the ego can give rise to the experience of the uniting force out of which the higher "I" works.

We're not trying to unite our thinking with the breathing, as was done in the case of the ancient mantras—but rather, we are separating our thinking and breathing. Breathing in, breathing out—and then, while holding the breath out, our attention goes to that center while we inwardly sound the words.

The more we understand what we are "sounding," the more powerful it will make the exercise. If I just use my common thinking to say in my head, "I am," then it's the same as chattering—but if I'm sounding "I am" from an inner connection with the reality of the words, then this will serve to organize this center. Inward sounding—or, as it is known in some schools, "vibrating"—means engaging all of our soul forces in the exercise. The thinking, feeling, and will must all be employed in the same direction, so that no other content enters the soul.

The next center is the "It thinks." When other human beings speak their thoughts, there are slight vibrations that occur in our own larynx as listeners—there are movements in our life body that occur around our own larynx. This may become ever clearer for us as this center is organized through the exercise; then we may recognize for ourselves what the effect of someone else's speech is on the surrounding world.

So, again, we breathe in for the same count as before—a count of two for the in-breath and four for the out-breath (or whatever number is comfortable to achieve)—and while the breath is held out, we focus all our attention upon the throat center while reverberating inwardly the words "It thinks." In the meditation, we don't think *about* the great cosmic thinking; we should not think *about* anything—instead, whatever lives in our soul through our understanding of these words will have its resonance in what we are speaking inwardly.

To awaken this center, we think "It thinks," with our whole being behind it.

The next point is at the heart center. The words are "She feels." We focus on the heart, but allow our attention to stream from the heart down the arms, and into the hands—working its way over into our hands while at the same time continuing to be present in the heart. Some may feel that their hands need to move apart as the streaming occurs. The movement of the arms should not be done by the meditant, but by the stream itself.

The next center is the center at the point of the navel. For this, we will concentrate on this point, but also on the whole "boundary" or skin surrounding the body, while sounding inwardly the words "He wills."

We can begin by doing this three times on each center, until we have the exercise working correctly—then, we need only do it once on each center.

At the end of the exercise, we let go of all the experiences connected to the body and then rest in empty consciousness (see *The Inner Work Path*).[34]

If achieving empty consciousness is not familiar to the meditant, then contemplating one's spiritual–divine ideal is also beneficial and serves to maintain the soul in the direction of the spirit until the meditation is complete.

Like all exercises arising out of the Mystery schooling, it can require several months, or even years, of working with the exercise before we really begin to understand the potency and transformative possibility of such exercises.

Most of the time, people will come to experience in this exercise that the "I am" brings a particular quality, and that the "It thinks" has a very different quality. It's very useful to learn to understand these different qualities. When streaming from the heart and into the arms and the hands, the "She feels" can bring about a bliss-like experience. This is just a faint taste of what can be experienced as rapture in certain spiritual encounters. It can be very tempting to stay with the "She feels" when this occurs. And yet, we have to then move to the "He wills," the creative force that allows us to give out to the world.

The mysteries of such an exercise can take many years to unfold. In time, we will begin to understand how it is that these words and experiences are necessary for any development toward our full humanity. And we will also begin to understand that these words and experiences have nothing to do with being in a particular bodily vehicle, but are given for all human beings alike.

The "She feels" reveals that it is related to our experience of what happens to us in our activity of forgetting the personal self—the state in which we allow the other to impress itself upon us. The "She" is this aspect of our being that can hear, that can experience, and that can be penetrated by the revelations of spiritual consciousness. As individuals, without the "She feels," we would be unable to directly experience the higher worlds, and through this, to gain direct knowledge and wisdom.

The "He wills" is the aspect that can "give forth" and unite with the activity of creating. It is our living remembering of the creative quality of the spiritual world.

> We must unite ourselves and become as one with higher truths. We must not only know them, but as a matter of course be able to administer them in living actions.... They must come to living expression in us; they must flow through us just as the functions of life flow through our organism. (Rudolf Steiner, *Knowledge of the Higher Worlds and Its Attainment*)[35]

So we can further differentiate this relationship between "I can take something in" and "I can bring something out into the world." It is an absolute necessity to be able to bring wisdom in such a way that it first comes in and through us, and then is given out into the world. It is the "He wills" that can transform the world we see. Because of the new spiritual task of our present age, if we treat human beings in such a way that we support them in cultivating only the "She feels" or only the "He wills," then a one-sidedness may arise that hinders them from re-enlivening the world.

Without the connection we all have with the spirit, we would only be a product of our upbringing. However, it is clear that the human being's capacities go beyond what has

been given to us by the outer world during our formati
years. And yet, our formation by the world has a definite
impact on what we will be able to unfold within ourselves, as
well as the ease with which we will be able to develop further.

The reality is that many children are not afforded the freedom to unfold their soul capacities equally and in a balanced
way. There are various ways that this development is limited
in our times. For example, it is certainly limited by placing on
children definitions of who they should be according to their
bodily vehicle. Some of us are limited in one direction and
others are limited in another. Some of us, in our intellectual
way of life, are being suppressed in both the "He wills" and
the "She feels." In this case, only experiences that cultivate
the "It thinks" are being given by the dominating intellectual
world, with activities that feed the thinking life alone.

It is up to individuals to recognize the imbalance living
within themselves—and, as adults, to do something about it
themselves. Meditation is an activity that brings us to a living
relationship with the spiritual world, and is a way to harmonize these imbalances.

> You are not a spiritual scientist merely by knowing about
> certain things. You are so only if you feel yourself within
> the spiritual world by virtue of this knowledge—if you
> know yourself quite definitely as a member of the spiri-
> tual world. (Rudolf Steiner, "On the Connection of the
> Living and the Dead")[36]

Living in this self-consciousness soul age, we need to be
able to elicit the wholeness of individuals and not impress
upon them anything that creates one-sided development in

them. Spiritually, we know what can result from such diversions (see chapter 1).

The effects are completely different if someone stands in front of a group of teenagers and says, "I'm going to call you all 'students,' so that you don't feel I am failing to see your diversity in terms of your various experiences of gender," out of some place of inner chatter—as compared with if we actually know the spiritual realities and effects of blocking the other's individuality, and the consequences this has on re-enlivening earthly life.

If we are only cultivating one-sided activities in the human being, we cannot create change in the direction of progressive spiritual unfolding. Our evolution is not a matter of static development but a continuous awakening. The potential is for the "I am" to awaken more and more every year, and with it, a greater capacity for "It thinks," with greater and deeper experiences of "She feels," and with a stronger feeling for the creative potential of "He wills."

If we want to transform how we live in the world, then it is useful to change our speech—not so that we can have empty chatter with new words, but because we want the fullness of the being of speech to be able to activate and re-enliven the world into the future.

The world is re-enlivened through us. The reason we don't want to treat people according to their vehicle, is that in doing so, we treat them according to one-sided capacities and implicitly encourage only that one-sided development. This has a profoundly detrimental effect when reflected into their spiritual development. Stuffing them with physical–material ideas of who they should be, telling them that they are only going to develop certain parts of themselves because of the body that they have—we can't afford to have this happening in the world anymore; we can't afford for the world to continue to die to the spiritual realities.

Every part in us that is liberated can in turn be used to liberate others. We're not trying to proclaim religious chatter, but to bring our being and everything we recognize to be true into the ground of our communion with the other— even in the smallest ways. "To be able to hear is to have opened the doors of the soul...to be able to speak is to have attained the power of helping others" (Mabel Collins, *Light on the Path*).[37]

Our meditative life might be personal, but our spiritual life belongs to others. We might not talk about what takes place in our meditation, but not to talk about what's really true to us inwardly...that is a matter of holding something back; it is declining to work with the Creator and the task of creating a better world.

If I experience the truth of spiritual life, but I am not able to transform this experience into something that I can then bring to the world, then has my inner activity served me in changing the outer world? Have I undertaken this inner work for myself—have I been tempted to remain shut up in my own enjoyment of spiritual insight? The overcoming of this temptation—that of enjoying for ourselves alone the fruits of spiritual life—starts with our ability to feel our humanity: feeling ourselves united with humanity from the "I am" through to the "He wills" that must necessarily follow.

We engage in meditation and inner practice so that we ourselves may experience the truth that is traced out in the spiritual world. But we are given experiences in our meditation *for the other*. By having direct experience of spiritual reality and direct revelations of spiritual life, our own soul is enriched and what we speak to the world will be enriched with spiritual forces. This is an ever-developing and evolving relationship. Slowly, gradually, we develop to have greater capacities, which we have received from spiritual realities, and that we may pass on to the world around us through our own thinking, feeling, and actions—and most certainly through our spoken words.

So what we may have spoken about five years ago, although still true, was never full enough. Now, when we reflect upon it five years later—and yet again at a later time—we can see that the fullness of truth in our souls has grown. We may think, "What I spoke back then was like speaking about a blade of grass, and now I'm seeing this whole field. How could I ever again talk about a blade of grass when now I see a whole field?" We give what we have at the moment; we can only give what is ours. The fact that it is not complete, and will still become something more in the future, is the living relationship at the center of this extraordinary Mystery of which we are a part.

What are esoterically known as the "draught of forgetfulness" and the "draught of remembrance,"[38] are like every aspect of the vortex of development—they grow within us through the cycles of the spiritual year. Forgetting is essential for experiencing; remembering is essential for sowing, for creating. I forget myself in order to remember God; and my activity of remembering God while living in the physical world re-enlivens the spirit in the world.

In everyday encounters, we are creating through what we give to the world. We can also see this quality enhanced in conversation. When two people are striving toward forgetting themselves and remembering the spiritual—receiving from the inner connection to the spirit in that moment and seeding it into the world—wondrous gifts are shared and grown. We have all felt how our words, seeded into the world, can uplift the other. It's because of such experiences that we feel the motivation to "seed the world." If we could have the biological drive toward procreation of the species living in our soul instead—that level of passion for change and transformation—then we would not need to suffer so much from the resistance to development, that lethargy that encumbers us from using all our forces toward humanity's spiritual progression.

When we are pushed into a one-sidedness in our development, then the realm of healthy sexuality becomes the kind of eroticism in which one seeks to gratify oneself and objectify the other—or it becomes the love of power and the desire for power over others.[39] The creative force that is expressed in the body as sexual energy then flows into these diversions instead of flowing into one's experience of deep interest in the world and the desire to bring about change in service to the needs of the world.

Even if the procreative forces that bring vibrancy into the body are weakened through the body's aging process, this ɛsn't stop our creative capacity, as the true transformative forces for seeding the world come through the soul. How many seeds live in us that we don't share? What would the world be like if we did share and plant the seeds of spiritual life from within our souls into the world around us?

> Love mediated by way of the senses is the wellspring of creative power, of what is coming into being. Without sense-borne love, nothing material would exist in the world; without spiritual love, nothing spiritual can arise in evolution. When we practice love, cultivate love, creative forces pour into the world. (Rudolf Steiner, *Love and Its Meaning in the World*)[40]

We can re-enliven what is dying by making use of the life of spiritual reality. It's not a higher spiritual being who does that—we do it. In and through us, we access the spirit in order to enliven this world. Toward this task, we are eternally supported by the spiritual beings of progression. All revelations that we receive are what they give to us; in return, what will we then give to the world?

All seeds of spiritual progress come from the divine spiritual world. The greatest thing we can do, once we have found the centered ground of our individual self, is to forget our personal selves, so that the revelations might speak into us. Then we can experience that in our interactions with the world. Even in the little things, we are remembering the spiritual world. In this way, we make holy our day, and we make whole the life around us. That is our creative task.

Notes

Some cited quotations in the text from translations of Rudolf Steiner's works have been modified to use gender-inclusive language.

1   Rudolf Steiner, *Education for Special Needs: The Curative Education Course*, CW 317, lect. June 25, 1924 (London: Rudolf Steiner Press, 2014). See also Rudolf Steiner, *Soul Economy: Body, Soul, and Spirit in Waldorf Education*, CW 303 (Great Barrington, MA: Anthroposophic Press, 2003).

2   See especially the chapter "The Present and Future of Cosmic and Human Evolution." Rudolf Steiner, *Occult Science: An Outline*, CW 13 (tr. G. and M. Adams, London: Rudolf Steiner Press, 1979); also translated as *An Outline of Occult Science* (tr. H. and L. Monges, Spring Valley, NY: Anthroposophic Press, 1972); and *An Outline of Esoteric Science* (tr. C. Creeger, Hudson, NY: Anthroposophic Press, 1993).

3   Rudolf Steiner, "Women and Society," lect. Nov. 17, 1906, Hamburg, CW 54 (London: Rudolf Steiner Press, 1985). Quoted from p. 74 in the compilation: *Sexuality, Love and Partnership from the Perspective of Spiritual Science. From the Work of Rudolf Steiner* (London: Rudolf Steiner Press, 2011, ed. M. Jonas).

4   Rudolf Steiner, "Man and Woman in the Light of Spiritual Science," lect. March 18, 1908 in Munich, CW 56. Published in English in *The Anthroposophical Review*, vol. 2, no. 1: 1980. Quoted from p. 45 in the compilation *Sexuality, Love and Partnership from the Perspective of Spiritual Science* (op. cit.).

5   Rudolf Steiner, *The Fall of the Spirits of Darkness*, lect. Oct. 26, 1917, Dornach, CW 177 (London: Rudolf Steiner Press, 1993), p. 185.

6   Rudolf Steiner, "Women and Society," lect. Nov. 17, 1906, CW 54 (op. cit.), p. 9f.

7   Rainer Maria Rilke, *Letters to a Young Poet* (tr. S. Mitchell, Merchant Books, 2012), p. 18.

8   Rudolf Steiner, *Kosmogonie*, CW 94, listeners' notes to a
     lect. June 30, 1906, Liepzig, as part of the series on "Popular
     Occultism" (Dornach: Rudolf Steiner Verlag, 1979), p. 143f.
     Published in English in *Love, Marriage, Sex: In the Light of
     Spiritual Science* (3 vols., 1970–1982): excerpts from Rudolf
     Steiner's work selected and translated by Richard Lewis.

9   See Rudolf Steiner, "Education for Adolescents," lect. June
     21, 1922, Stuttgart, CW 302b. First published in *Journal for
     Anthroposophy*, spring 1979.

10   See especially *Knowledge of the Higher Worlds*, "Some Effects
     of Initiation"; *An Outline of Esoteric Science*, "Knowledge
     of the Higher Worlds—Initiation"; and *Guidance in Esoteric
     Training*, part 1: "General Requirements" (pp. 13–19). Rudolf
     Steiner, *Knowledge of the Higher Worlds: How is It Achieved?*
     CW 10 (tr. rev. by D. Osmond and C. Davy, London: Rudolf
     Steiner Press, 1993); also translated as *Knowledge of the Higher
     Worlds and Its Attainment* (tr. revised by H. and L. Mon-
     ges, Anthroposophic Press, 1947), and *How to Know Higher
     Worlds* (tr. C. Bamford, Hudson, NY: Anthroposophic Press,
     1994). Rudolf Steiner, *Occult Science: An Outline*, CW 13 (op.
     cit.); also translated as *An Outline of Occult Science* (op. cit.),
     and *An Outline of Esoteric Science* (op. cit.). Rudolf Steiner,
     CW 245, *Guidance in Esoteric Training: From the Esoteric
     School* (London: Rudolf Steiner Press, 1994).

11   Rudolf Steiner, "Women and Society," lect. Nov. 17, 1906,
     CW 54 (op. cit.). Quotation adapted from p. 73 in the compi-
     lation *Sexuality, Love and Partnership from the Perspective of
     Spiritual Science* (ed. M. Jonas, op. cit.).

12   Rudolf Steiner, *Intuitive Thinking as a Spiritual Path: A Phi-
     losophy of Freedom*, CW 4, ch. 14, "Individuality and Genus"
     (tr. M. Lipson, Anthroposophic Press, 1995), p. 228f.

13   Rudolf Steiner, lect. Aug. 23, 1922, Oxford, "The Organization
     of the Waldorf School." In *The Spiritual Ground of Education*,
     CW 305 (Great Barrington, MA: Anthroposophic Press, 2004),
     p. 99.

14   *Open Secret: Versions of Rumi* (tr. J. Moyne and C. Barks,
     Boston: Shambhala, 1999), Quatrain no. 158, p. 8.

15   Daniel Ladinsky (ed.), *Love Poems from God: Twelve Sacred
     Voices from the East and West* (New York: Penguin, 2002),
     p. 47.

16   This is described in the male/female sections of the *EduCareDo* anthroposophical distance education lessons.

17   D. Ladinsky (ed.), *Love Poems from God* (op. cit.), p. 52.

18   Ibid., p. 39.

19   Rudolf Steiner, "How to Listen to the Spirit," lect. June 12, 1919, Heidenheim, CW 193, published in *The Meaning of Life and other Lectures on Fundamental Issues* (London: Rudolf Steiner Press, 1999).

20   Rudolf Steiner, *Geisteswissenschaftliche Menschenkunde*, lect. Oct. 26, 1908, Berlin, CW 107 (Dornach: Rudolf Steiner Verlag, 1988), p. 65. This translation adapted from the version by M. Gotfare, 1984, *The Astral World*, lect. 3, "The Law of the Astral Plane: Renunciation; the Law of the Devachanic Plane: Sacrifice."

21   Rudolf Steiner, "How to Listen to the Spirit," lect. June 12, 1919, CW 193, in *The Meaning of Life*, op. cit.

22   Rainer Maria Rilke, *Letters to a Young Poet* (op. cit.), letter #4, 16 July 1903.

23   Rudolf Steiner, "How to Listen to the Spirit," lect. June 12, 1919, CW 193, in *The Meaning of Life*, op. cit.

24   Rudolf Steiner, CW 10, *Knowledge of the Higher Worlds and Its Attainment* (op. cit.), "Initiation," p. 96; also printed as *Knowledge of the Higher Worlds: How is it Achieved?* (op. cit., p. 90), and *How to Know Higher Worlds* (op. cit.).

25   Rudolf Steiner, "From Empty Phrase to Living Word," lect. June 8, 1919, Stuttgart, CW 192, printed in *Whitsun and Ascension: An Introductory Reader* (London: Rudolf Steiner Press, 2007), p. 80f.

26   Rudolf Steiner, "From Empty Phrase to Living Word," lect. June 8, 1919, CW 192, in *Whitsun and Ascension*, ibid., p. 78f.

27   Rudolf Steiner, "How to Listen to the Spirit," lect. June 12, 1919, CW 193, in *The Meaning of Life* (op. cit.).

28   Daniel Ladinsky (ed.), *A Year with Hafiz: Daily Contemplations* (Penguin, 2011), entry of June 6, "Energy in Sounds."

29   Rudolf Steiner, "From Empty Phrase to Living Word," lect. June 8, 1919, CW 192, in *Whitsun and Ascension* (op. cit.).

30   Quoted in *Rudolf Steiner, Finding the Greater Self: Meditations for Harmony and Healing* (ed. M. Barton, London: Rudolf Steiner Press, 2002), p. 61.

31 From Rudolf Steiner, *Guidance in Esoteric Training: From the Esoteric School,* CW 245 (op. cit.), pp. 32ff.

32 Lisa Romero, *The Inner Work Path: A Foundation for Meditative Practice in the Light of Anthroposophy* (Great Barrington, MA: SteinerBooks, 2014). The others books in this series are *Developing the Self through the Inner Work Path in the Light of Anthroposophy* (2015), and *Living Inner Development: The Necessity of True Inner Development in the Light of Anthroposophy* (2016).

33 Verse by Rudolf Steiner, *Rudolf Steiner: Finding the Greater Self* (op. cit.), p. 61.

34 Lisa Romero, *The Inner Work Path* (op. cit.). See also *Developing the Self* and *Living Inner Development* (op. cit.).

35 This translation adapted from Rudolf Steiner, CW 10, *Knowledge of the Higher Worlds and Its Attainment* (op. cit.), "Initiation," p. 96f; also printed as *Knowledge of the Higher Worlds: How is it Achieved?* (op. cit., p. 91), and *How to Know Higher Worlds: A Modern Path of Initiation* (op. cit.).

36 Rudolf Steiner, "On the Connection of the Living and the Dead," lect. Nov. 9, 1916, Bern, CW 168.

37 Mabel Collins, *Light on the Path* (Pasadena, CA: Theosophical University Press, 1997), "Note on Sect. 2," p. 24.

38 See Rudolf Steiner, CW 10, *Knowledge of the Higher Worlds and Its Attainment* (op. cit.) "Initiation."

39 See further in Rudolf Steiner, "Education for Adolescents," lect. June 21, 1922, CW 302b (op. cit.).

40 Rudolf Steiner, "Love and Its Meaning in the World," lect. Dec. 17, 1912, Zurich, CW 143, printed in, Rudolf Steiner, *Love and Its Meaning in the World* (Hudson, NY: Anthroposophic Press, 1998), p. 182.

"Lisa Romero has been working at Cape Byron Rudolf Steiner School for ten years, bringing age-appropriate guidance to every high school student through class lessons and individual and small group sessions. Lisa expertly covers all areas of gender and sexuality from an anthroposophical perspective, strongly meeting the current world of the teenager in navigating the sensitive issues of gender and sexuality in an increasingly complex world of social media. In conjunction with this, she speaks with the parents and offers professional development for the teachers and school staff in this subject. Lisa's work is of enormous benefit to our school, complementing educative practices included in Main Lessons and in our Student Wellbeing program. Students feel supported and empowered by her time with them, and there is no doubt that they make better decisions and are healthier for her work with them."

Katie Biggin,
High School Principal and English Teacher,
Cape Byron Rudolf Steiner School

LISA ROMERO is the author of several books on inner development, a complementary health practitioner, and an adult educator who offers health care and education enriched by Anthroposophy since 1993. From 2006, the primary focus of her work has been on teaching inner development and anthroposophical meditation. Through the *Inner Work Path,* Lisa offers lectures, courses, and retreats for personal and professional development, in communities and schools worldwide.

For many years, Lisa was the lecturer of Health and Nutrition and Male/Female studies at Sydney Rudolf Steiner College, where she continues to give lectures on inner development to the tutors.

Since 1999, she has been presenting on the subject of gender, sexuality, and spiritual life. She has been working with Waldorf schools as part of their "health and wellbeing" curriculum, working directly with the students, teachers, and parents on this theme. Lisa has contributed to and is an adviser for the "Health and Personal Development for the Australian Steiner Curriculum Framework." She has developed training courses and facilitates professional development on this subject for teachers and health professionals.

Lisa designed and facilitated *EduCareDo* "Towards Health and Healing," which has offered eight-year courses focused on working with therapists from all modalities, as well as Waldorf teachers, toward cultivating the depth of anthroposophic insight through practical applications of therapeutic and pedagogical methods.

Lisa is a contributor, tutor, and director of *Inner Work Path, EduCareDo, Developing the Self—Developing the World,* and the *Y Project. EduCareDo* is an organization facilitating long-distance, self-awakening study in the foundations of Anthroposophy. *Developing the Self—Developing the World* offers community education, and the Y Project supports the transition of young people into healthy community life.

For meditation courses and talks,
see innerworkpath.com.

For more information on Sex and Gender
Education, see developingtheself.org.

CPSIA information can be obtained
at www.ICGtesting.com
Printed in the USA
BVHW031709150319
542793BV00001B/108/P

9 781621 481911